Thracian
Sea
MW01259082
AEGEAN
SEA
TURKEY
NORTH AEGEAN
ISLANDS
UBOEAN
SLANDS
CYCLADES
DODECANESE
Sea Of Crete
CRETAN ISLANDS

The Greek Islands Cookbook

THIS BOOK IS DEDICATED TO
MY MOTHER TESI, WITH LOVE.

—

Carolina Doriti

The Greek Islands Cookbook

murdoch books
London | Sydney

RECIPE NOTES

Eggs are always medium (UK)/large (Aus/US).
Butter is always unsalted.
Herbs are always fresh, unless specified otherwise.
Both metric and imperial measurements are used in this book. Follow one set of measurements throughout, not a mixture, as they are not necessarily interchangeable.
All spoon measurements are level, unless specified otherwise.
Tablespoon measures: we have used 15ml (3 teaspoon) tablespoon measures.

—

Published in 2025 by Murdoch Books,
an imprint of Allen & Unwin

Murdoch Books UK
Ormond House
26–27 Boswell Street
London WC1N 3JZ
Phone: +44 (0) 20 8785 5995
murdochbooks.co.uk
info@murdochbooks.co.uk

Murdoch Books Australia
Cammeraygal Country
83 Alexander Street
Crows Nest NSW 2065
Phone: +61 (0)2 8425 0100
murdochbooks.com.au
info@murdochbooks.com.au

For corporate orders and custom publishing,
contact our business development team at
salesenquiries@murdochbooks.com.au

Publisher: Céline Hughes
Project Editor: Lisa Pendreigh
Cover and Text Designer: Studio Polka
Photographer: Manos Chatzikonstantis
Food Stylist: Carolina Doriti
Props Stylists: Carolina Doriti and Manos Chatzikonstantis
Head of Production, UK: Lauren Fulbright
Production Director, Australia: Lou Playfair

Murdoch Books Australia acknowledges the Traditional Owners of the Country on which we live and work. We pay our respects to all Aboriginal and Torres Strait Islander Elders, past and present.

ISBN 978 1 7615 00763

A catalogue record for this book is available from the British Library

A catalogue record for this book is available from the National Library of Australia

Colour reproduction by Born Group, London, UK

Printed by 1010 Printing International Limited, China

10 9 8 7 6 5 4 3 2 1

CONTENTS

INTRODUCTION

Nestled at the crossroads of Europe, Asia and Africa, the Greek islands offer a captivating array of landscapes, sculpted by the vast, shimmering seas that surround them. Picture yourself wandering these sun-kissed gems, where the Aegean, Ionian and Libyan Seas have inspired ancient myths and vibrant traditions. The Greek islanders, deeply connected to the sea, have lovingly named various parts of the Aegean – Cretan, Karpathian, Icarian, Myrtoan and Thracian – with each name reflecting their profound sense of ownership and intimate bond with the waters that lap their home shores.

As someone enchanted by the magic of the Greek islands, writing this cookbook has been a heartfelt journey of love and discovery. My grandfather, George, with whom I was very close, hailed from the Cycladic island of Paros and was a passionate storyteller and food lover. I spent countless hours listening to his stories and journeying back in time with him. I have spent every summer of my life on these islands, tasting their local produce and recipes while witnessing their evolution through tourism. Preserving the islands' natural beauty and cherished traditions has become increasingly important to me, as it is to many locals.

My fascination with Greek island cuisine began as a personal adventure, exploring each island's unique culinary traditions and meeting local cooks and producers over the years. Intertwined with fond memories of carefree holidays, the richness and simplicity of island recipes never ceases to enthral me. This book is more than just a collection of recipes; it's a tribute to the vibrant cultures and passionate people who have generously shared their food secrets and stories with me and the wonderful local flavours I have savoured. Each page celebrates the warmth of the Greek islanders, their deep connection to the land and sea, and their remarkable and highly sustainable culinary creativity, which keeps evolving and inspiring cooks. Through these recipes, I hope to transport you to sunlit shores, busy fishing ports, bustling markets, cosy home kitchens and welcoming tavernas, where the aromas and flavours weave stories of community, heritage and joy.

Imagine the Greek islands as a dazzling scattering of jewels across azure seas. There are around 6,000 islands and islets, with about 227 inhabited, each possessing a unique charm. This rich tapestry of microcultures reflects fascinating histories and traditions manifesting in everything from local arts to exquisite cuisines. Wood carving, marble sculpting, ceramics, weaving and music are just a few of the artistic expressions that bring the islands' heritage to life. The culinary traditions of the islands are shaped by their geography as well as their history – each landscape influences what can be grown, farmed or sourced locally. Island cuisine reflects the bounty of the land and sea – from high mountains and lush valleys to rugged coastlines and rocky grounds – and the constraints of remote living. Some islands have benefited from historical trade routes, bringing ideas and ingredients, such as spices, that set their dishes apart. Others have remained more influenced by long-standing local practices. This combination of isolation and connectivity has led to both shared culinary themes and distinct regional flavours.

Geographically, the Greek islands are divided into six distinct clusters, each with its own unique landscape and offering a distinct taste of Greek cuisine and culture:

+ THE IONIAN ISLANDS to the west include Corfu, Kefalonia, Ithaca, Zakynthos, Lefkada, Paxi and Kythira, closer to the Aegean. They are known for their verdant landscapes and Venetian heritage, reflected in the architecture, gardens and cuisine that blends local ingredients with sophisticated spices.

+ THE CYCLADES – from *kyklos*, meaning 'circle' – form a picturesque cluster of islands in the Aegean. This group includes Santorini, Serifos, Folegandros, Amorgos and Sifnos, all known for a rugged beauty, iconic whitewashed buildings and breathtaking sunsets. Volcanic soil nurtures exceptional wines, while vibrant herbs add flavour to a local cuisine that embraces simplicity and seasonality.

+ THE NORTH-EASTERN AEGEAN ISLANDS includes Lesvos, Chios, Samos and Limnos. These islands offer a sensory experience, from exploring lush green landscapes to diving into lively cultural festivals, such as the Ikarian *panigyria* (see page 86). The local cuisine, mostly on the bigger islands, is enriched by the food of refugees from Asia Minor. Some of the delightful produce deriving from these islands includes ouzo, *mastiha* (see page 182) and an array of citrus fruits, cheeses and seafood.

+ THE DODECANESE ISLANDS are composed of Rhodes, Kos, Astypalea and Karpathos. They combine historic grandeur with natural beauty. Medieval ruins are set against idyllic beaches. Traditional dishes feature bulgur (cracked) wheat, chickpeas (garbanzo beans) and other beans, alongside stuffed vegetables. Many recipes are spiced with cumin. The cuisine here shares traits with the Cyclades and Crete, with similar vegetable or chickpea fritters, cheeses, breads, pasta, pies and sweet pastries.

+ CRETE, the largest and southernmost island, stands as a cornerstone of Greek culinary tradition. Surrounded by the Aegean Sea to the north and the Libyan Sea to the south, Crete is celebrated for its ancient cuisine and exceptional local produce. From olive oil, cheese and cured pork to wine and honey, Crete's food reflects its land. Dishes feature snails, *xinochondros* (fermented pasta), breads, rusks and a bounty of vegetables and fruits, from classic Greek produce to avocados and bananas.

+ THE SARONIC ISLANDS – Salamina, Aegina, Hydra, Spetses and Poros, near Athens – are treasured for their neoclassical charm and vibrant cultural life. With a focus on seafood, dishes often include local delights such as Aegina's pistachios, Poros' lemons and Hydra's famous almond treats.

+ EVIA, the second-largest Greek island, has a landscape ranging from high mountains and fertile valleys to sandy beaches. Evia provides nearby parts of mainland Greece with dairy, meat, seafood and fresh produce, including figs and mushrooms. Its cuisine blends mainland Greek and Sporades influences.

+ THE SPORADES ISLANDS, including Skiathos, Skyros, Alonissos and Skopelos, captivate with their dense forests and crystal-clear waters. Alonissos hosts Greece's first marine park, a sanctuary for the endangered Mediterranean monk seal. The cuisine is a celebration of exceptional seafood, featuring prawns, langoustines, lobster and the prized Alonissos tuna. Local favourites include a spiral-shaped fried pie. Skopelos is known for its delicious prunes and high-quality goat meat (see page 42).

From the majestic mountains and lush forests of Evia, Crete, Kefalonia and Samothraki to the volcanic splendour of Santorini, Milos and Nisyros, the Greek islands offer a breathtaking range of contrasting land and sea. On some islands, where farming has traditionally thrived or where winds made sea travel unreliable, the cuisine is centred around hearty meats, fresh local produce, pulses and grains, with seafood playing a lesser role. Islands like Tinos, Andros, Kos and Crete exemplify this agricultural richness. In contrast, islands such as Kalymnos, Symi, Kastelorizo and Antiparos have nurtured a deep connection to the sea as other local resources were historically more limited. Here, vibrant fishing traditions shape the cuisine, with fresh seafood taking centre stage and the surrounding waters are a lifeline, influencing daily life and culinary practices.

Historically, islanders produced as much as they could locally, preserving everything that could be preserved, from wild herbs, capers and sea fennel to tomatoes, nuts, fruit, bread and milk. Despite their isolation, these islands maintained contact with the entire Mediterranean through sea trade, creating a chain of exchange to supply goods. When tourism became the main source of income for islanders, local production gradually dropped on some islands. However, people continued these practices, maintaining their recipes and traditions. In the last years, there has been a significant effort to revive local production.

Most islands boast fantastic cheeses and wines, many of which have recently gained wider recognition. Cheeses, as well as recipes across islands, can be quite similar, although sometimes different names are used locally. Pies, both sweet and savoury, are very popular everywhere – each island makes their own styles of pies, with local filo (phyllo) recipes, featuring their local cheeses or foraged greens. Naturally, historically poorer islands such as Anafi and Kimolos have simpler recipes with fewer ingredients, while more cosmopolitan islands like Chios and Syros offer complex dishes as well, with a richer and more diverse cuisine.

The diet of many Greek islanders is held up as an ideal Mediterranean diet, promoting longevity and well-being. The traditional diets of Crete and Ikaria are prime examples, featuring abundant vegetables, fruits, olive oil, pulses, herbal teas, high-quality cheeses, free-range eggs and, of course, wine. Meat was traditionally enjoyed less frequently, reserved for special occasions and Sundays. Traditional feasts, both in the Aegean and Ionian islands, often centre around meat dishes such as chicken, pork and goat, plus on certain occasions fish. Foraging and preserving – whether for sea salt, herbs, snails or wild fruits – are integral to traditional island cooking. Though overfishing is a concern, the islands still offer amazing seafood, with dishes featuring whole fish, shellfish, lobsters, octopus and squid. Traditional methods of preserving fish and seafood are still very popular, such as salted sardines, marinated anchovies, sun-dried mackerel, and delicacies like the smoked swordfish of Kalymnos or the jarred tuna fillets of Alonissos. Each island's preserved seafood, often enjoyed with local spirits, adds a special touch to their culinary heritage and the social aspect of it… sharing.

Whether enjoyed in a charming village taverna or a bustling family kitchen, the flavours and stories of the Greek islands continue to enchant and inspire. This book invites you on a culinary journey through these cherished islands, showcasing their idyllic landscapes and vibrant recipes. Each island's character shines through its unique array of flavours, offering a celebration of Greek culinary heritage and the communities that preserve these traditions. May this journey inspire you to explore, taste and embrace the magic of the Greek islands and their delightful recipes. This book has been a labour of love. It is a bridge from the Greek islands to your kitchen, inviting you to experience the same wonder and delight that has touched not only my senses, but also my heart.

Breakfast & Brunch

CHAPTER 1

Fourtalia **Eggs with sausages, potatoes and mint**

FROM **THE CYCLADES**

SERVES 2–4

- 3 medium potatoes (such as Maris Piper, Russet, Yukon Gold or any other variety good for frying), peeled
- 2 thick rustic sausages (about 180g/6oz, spicy ones work well too)
- Olive oil or any other neutral oil, for frying
- 6 large free-range eggs
- 2 tablespoons chopped fresh mint leaves, plus extra to serve
- Salt and freshly ground black pepper

TO SERVE (OPTIONAL)

- Crumbled feta

Fourtalia (also called *froutalia*) originates from the Cycladic islands, particularly Andros, Tinos and Mykonos, renowned for their gusty winds and pork-rich diets. This humble omelette is intertwined with the traditional pig-slaughter season, a practice still observed in certain villages. The original recipe includes preserved pork or sausage and lard, staples in every household. The sausage typically used is rustic and robust, infused with thyme, aniseed, fennel, black pepper, orange and wine. Similar to a frittata, potatoes form the base and occasionally artichokes, broad (fava) beans or onions are added, ensuring a low-cost, satisfying meal. I've opted for a lighter dish by omitting any cheese and milk, which is quicker and simpler to prepare but just as delicious. Plus I prefer crispier potatoes! For a vegetarian option, replace the sausages with courgettes (zucchini). Greeks relish sharing this dish during leisurely conversation, and even over drinks as it is good at any time of day, not just for brunch.

Cut the potatoes into rough 1.5cm (½ inch) cubes. Place them in a bowl of cold water with a pinch of salt and let them soak for 15 minutes. Drain in a colander and pat dry with paper towels.

Meanwhile, slice the sausages into 1cm (⅓ inch) thick rounds. Heat a large, deep, non-stick frying pan (skillet) with a lid over a medium heat and drizzle in a little oil. Once hot, add the sliced sausages and cook for a few minutes, turning occasionally, until lightly browned on all sides. Leaving any oil behind in the pan, transfer the sausages to a plate and keep warm.

Using the same pan, add enough oil to reach a depth of 3cm (1 inch) to cover the potatoes. Turn up the heat to medium-high. Once the oil reaches 180°C/350°F, add the diced potatoes and fry until crisp and golden – this typically takes 8–12 minutes depending on the variety of potato. For the first 6–7 minutes, avoid stirring the potatoes to allow them to cook evenly. Once they start to crisp up, gently stir to ensure even cooking.

While the potatoes are frying, crack the eggs into a bowl, add the mint and season with plenty of salt and black pepper. Lightly beat until just combined.

Once the potatoes are crispy, carefully ladle or pour off some of the oil (about ⅓ cup) from the pan. Return the pan to a medium-low heat. Arrange the cooked sausages over the potatoes in the pan and pour over the beaten eggs. Cover with the lid and cook for 6 minutes, or until the eggs are set.

Using a spatula, transfer the *fourtalia* to a serving platter. Sprinkle over the crumbled feta, if using, immediately before serving.

Sfakianes pites **Cheese-stuffed pancakes**

FROM **CRETE**

MAKES 12

260g (9½oz) plain (all-purpose) flour, plus extra for rolling
1 tablespoon olive oil
Pinch of salt
1 teaspoon fresh lemon juice
Around 120–150ml (4–5fl oz) water, at room temperature
240–250g (8½–9oz) *mizithra* or fresh ricotta (for an excellent alternative to *mizithra*, blend ricotta with a tangy goats' cheese or fresh chèvre)

TO SERVE (OPTIONAL)
Honey, for drizzling
Ground cinnamon, for dusting
Ground walnuts or toasted sesame seeds, for sprinkling

One of Crete's culinary gems is this stuffed pancake, filled with fennel fronds mixed with spring onions (scallions) or a fresh cheese. Cretans are famed for their cheese-making, from fresh, creamy cheeses to hard cheeses aged in caves. Particularly known for the cheese-stuffed pancake is Sfakia, a village in south-western Crete, popular for its remote beaches. The pancake is filled with their local *galomizithra*, a PDO tangy, creamy cheese crafted from ewes' or goats' milk. Alternatively, sour or sweet *mizithra*, as well as fresh ricotta, can be used as a substitute. Once cooked, the pancake is drizzled with honey, but to further elevate the dish, sprinkle a little ground cinnamon, ground walnuts or toasted sesame seeds on top. For an adventurous touch, consider adding other nuts, seeds or spices, like a pinch of chilli. These pancakes make great snacks and if served plain can be enjoyed with a salad or soup instead of bread. When served this way, you could always add some black pepper or chopped herbs to the cheese filling.

In the bowl of an electric stand mixer fitted with the hook attachment, combine the flour, oil, salt and lemon juice. Mix at medium speed until just combined. While mixing, gradually pour in the water and knead at medium speed for 5 minutes or until the dough is soft, smooth, but not too sticky. If necessary, add a tiny bit of flour to prevent it from sticking. Shape the dough into a ball, place it in a bowl, cover the bowl with a clean dish towel and let it rest for 1 hour.

Meanwhile, cream the cheese in a bowl using a fork – it must be as smooth as possible so it doesn't tear the dough. Shape the cheese into 12 small balls, each weighing around 20g (¾oz) and set aside.

Divide the dough into 12 equal pieces, each weighing around 70g (2½oz), then shape into balls. On a lightly floured work surface, press the first ball down and sprinkle it with a little flour. Using a floured rolling pin, lightly roll the dough out into a rough 8cm (3 inch) disc. Place a cheese ball in its centre and lift the dough up and around the cheese to enclose. Roll it again in your palm to seal in the cheese and then set aside. Continue with the remaining dough and cheese.

Once finished, lightly flour the work surface and rolling pin. Gently roll out the first ball into a 12cm (5 inch) disc without tearing it. Carefully place it on a clean dish towel and keep covered while you repeat with the remaining dough.

Place a non-stick pan over a medium heat. Once hot, lightly brush with olive oil. Cook the first pancake for 1–2 minutes on each side until golden, then flip and cook on the first side for a further 1 minute. Repeat with the remaining pancakes.

The classic way to serve these pancakes is drizzled with honey and with some ground cinnamon, ground walnuts or toasted sesame seeds sprinkled over, if you like. You can also serve these plain, either warm or at room temperature.

Koskosela **Scrambled eggs in aubergine and tomato sauce**

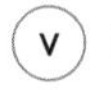 

FROM **SANTORINI**

SERVES 2–4

1 aubergine (eggplant, about 280g/10oz), peeled
2 tablespoons olive oil
950g (2lb 2oz) ripe tomatoes, grated (shredded)
1–2 fresh thyme sprigs (or use 1 teaspoon dried thyme)
5 large free-range eggs, beaten
100g (3½oz) feta, crumbled
1 tablespoon chopped fresh basil, plus extra to serve
1½ tablespoons capers, drained, rinsed and dried
Salt and freshly ground black pepper

TO SERVE
Slices of toasted bread

Scrambled eggs in tomato sauce with feta (or other local cheeses) is a quintessential summer dish enjoyed throughout Greece. Known as *strapatsada* in most of the country, *kayiana* in parts of the Peloponnese, and *koskosela* in the Cycladic islands, it boasts regional variations that add to its charm. On Santorini, diced aubergines (eggplants) are added, especially the island's famed white variety, known for its sweetness and fewer seeds due to its volcanic origin. While recommended if available, regular aubergines work just as well. You can enrich the sauce with other vegetables found in your fridge, such as courgettes (zucchini) or peas. This dish is served at all times of the day thanks to its quick preparation, balanced nutrition and irresistible taste. Its versatility means it is delightful on toasted bread or in sandwiches, making a convenient and satisfying brunch for any relaxed occasion.

Using the large holes of a box grater, grate (shred) the aubergine into a bowl.

Place a large pan over a medium-high heat and add the oil. Once hot, add the grated aubergine to the pan with a pinch of salt and cook, stirring continuously, for 2–3 minutes or until the aubergine has softened.

Next, add the grated tomatoes and thyme, along with salt and pepper to taste. Allow the sauce to simmer, stirring occasionally, for about 15–20 minutes (this will depend on how juicy the tomatoes are). The sauce is ready when it has thickened and there is very little excess liquid left.

Once the tomato sauce has thickened, gently stir in the beaten eggs. Keeping the heat at medium to prevent overcooking the eggs, let the eggs sit in the pan for a few seconds to start to set and then cook, while stirring with a spatula as though scrambling the eggs, for about 2 minutes.

When the eggs are almost cooked, fold in the crumbled feta and chopped basil. Remove the pan from heat.

Serve the scrambled eggs in the sauce topped with the capers and some extra basil, if you like, and seasoned with plenty of black pepper. For a hearty brunch, serve some toasted bread alongside.

TIP
If you can't get good ripe tomatoes, use sweet cherry tomatoes instead and blitz them in a food processor.

Katimeria **Fluffy pancakes with honey, walnuts and cinnamon or Quick-cook flatbreads**

FROM **SAMOS**

MAKES 25

500g (1lb 2oz) plain (all-purpose) flour
9g (⅓oz) instant dried yeast
½ teaspoon fine sea salt
½ teaspoon caster (superfine) sugar
1 tablespoon olive oil, plus extra for greasing your hands
120–150ml (4–5fl oz) whole (full-fat) milk
300g (10½oz) strained Greek-style yogurt
Oil, for frying

Though Greek pancakes, generally known as *tiganites*, grace tables across the islands with their own regional twists and local names, the *katimeria* from Samos stand out as something truly special. Around the different islands the term *katimeria* is used to refer to different treats, usually fried cheese pies, but on this island, *katimeria* take on a unique form. They're crafted from a soft dough enriched with yeast or sourdough and yogurt, then shaped into flat disks and fried. As they cook, they magically puff up into airy, hollow balls, making them incredibly exciting and versatile.

The *katimeria* can be filled with either savoury or sweet fillings, from cheese and ham or hummus to jam, praline or ice cream. For a special breakfast, they pair beautifully with fresh fruit and yogurt or simply drizzled with honey and finished with ground cinnamon and chopped nuts. But here's where it gets even more interesting: with the same dough, you can take a different route. Instead of frying, you can opt to grill the disks in a dry, non-stick pan until golden, transforming them into flatbreads. These versatile flatbreads can be shaped larger and used as pita wraps for souvlaki and other sandwiches, offering endless possibilities for more culinary creativity!

In the bowl of an electric stand mixer fitted with the hook attachment, combine the flour, yeast, salt, sugar and olive oil. Mix on medium-high speed for 5 minutes or until the ingredients are well combined.

While mixing on medium speed, gradually pour in 120ml (4fl oz) of the milk. Next, add the yogurt and mix until the dough is well combined, smooth and just slightly sticky without leaving your hands dirty. If necessary, adjust the consistency of the dough by adding a little extra milk or flour, one teaspoon at a time.

Lightly grease your hands with olive oil and shape the dough into a ball, coating it lightly with the oil from your hands – you don't want it too oily. Place the dough in a bowl, cover it with a clean dish towel and leave to rise for about 1 hour or until it doubles in size.

Once the dough has risen, lightly grease your hands again with more olive oil. Divide the dough into small balls, each roughly the size of a walnut. Using a rolling pin, roll each ball out into a thin flat disk, about 10–12cm (4–5 inches) in diameter. Place the disks on a clean dish towel, covering them with another towel to prevent them from drying out. For best results, let them stand covered for 15–20 minutes, however if you're short on time, you can proceed to cooking them in one of the following ways:

Recipe continues overleaf

FOR FLUFFY PANCAKES

Pour enough sunflower oil, about 5cm (2 inch) depth, into a heavy-based pot and place it over a medium-high heat. Once the oil is hot, add the first dough disk. It will puff up into a ball; flip it over and fry for about 1–2 minutes or until golden – if necessary, turn the heat down to medium if the oil gets too hot. Transfer the cooked pancake to a plate lined with paper towels to absorb any excess oil. Repeat with the remaining dough disks, frying one or two at a time depending on the size of the pan. Serve the pancakes drizzled with honey, dusted with cinnamon and sprinkled with ground walnuts.

FOR QUICK-COOK FLATBREADS

Heat a large non-stick pan over a medium-high heat. Once hot, add a couple of dough disks at a time to the dry pan (depending on their size and the size of the pan). Cook for about 1 minute on each side or until golden and fluffy – if necessary, turn the heat down to medium if the pan gets too hot. Serve the flatbreads with your choice of savoury or sweet dips or sides.

Island-inspired granola with yogurt, fruit and honey

FROM **THE ISLANDS**

MAKES 1 X 1.5-LITRE/ 50FL-OZ JAR

- 50g (1¾oz) unroasted pistachios, chopped
- 100g (3½oz) unroasted almonds, chopped
- 20g (¾oz) untoasted sesame seeds
- 1 heaped tablespoon poppy seeds
- 150g (5½oz) unroasted buckwheat
- 200g (7oz) rolled oats
- 1 teaspoon orange zest (unwaxed)
- ½ teaspoon lemon zest (unwaxed)
- 60ml (2fl oz) olive oil
- 90g (3oz) runny raw honey (or use agave syrup if vegan)
- 2 heaped teaspoons tahini or almond butter
- ½ teaspoon vanilla extract
- 1 teaspoon ground cinnamon
- ½ teaspoon sea salt
- 2 fresh thyme sprigs
- 50g (1¾oz) dried figs, chopped
- 50g (1¾oz) dried prunes, chopped
- 50g (1¾oz) dried blackcurrants or small raisins

TO SERVE

- Strained Greek-style yogurt (or coconut yogurt, chia pudding or nut milk, if vegan)
- Honey (or agave syrup, if vegan)
- Fresh fruit of your choice
- Bee pollen (optional)

Greek yogurt is already a breakfast favourite, but with a little flair, it becomes a morning masterpiece. Inspired by the diverse bounty of nuts and fruits that flourishes across the Greek islands – think Aegina's pistachios, Zante's currants, Lemnos' sesame and tahini, Skopelos' prunes, the citrus of Chios and Evia's figs – this fragrant, nutritious granola is the perfect match for creamy yogurt. Infused with the essence of the Greek islands, it boasts hints of citrus, cinnamon and thyme. I like to top it with fresh fruit as well, especially figs or berries, a little extra honey and some bee pollen. If you find yourself exploring the Greek islands, be sure to keep an eye out for locally crafted yogurt from island cooperatives or small producers. It's an experience not to be missed, especially when paired with the local honey.

Preheat the oven to 150°C/130°C fan/300°F/gas 2. Line a large baking tray with parchment paper.

In a large bowl, combine the chopped pistachios and almonds with the sesame seeds, poppy seeds, buckwheat, oats and orange zest and lemon zest.

In a separate bowl, whisk together the olive oil, honey, tahini or almond butter, vanilla extract, cinnamon and salt until well combined. If the mixture is too thick to mix well, warm it over a very low heat. Pour this mixture into the bowl with the nuts, seeds and oats and mix thoroughly. You can use your hands (wearing gloves) or a silicone spatula for this step.

Spread the granola mixture evenly over the prepared baking tray using a silicone spatula, then tuck in the thyme sprigs.

Bake in the hot oven for about 25 minutes, stirring halfway through, until the granola turns golden. Once done, allow the granola to cool completely before removing and discarding the thyme sprigs. Mix in all the dried fruit.

When stored in an airtight container in a dry place, the granola can be kept for up to 2 weeks.

To serve it with yogurt, make sure the yogurt is well strained before spooning it in a bowl. Sprinkle a generous amount of granola over the yogurt, followed by a drizzle of honey and your favourite fruits. Finish it off, if you like, with a sprinkling of bee pollen. Serve immediately.

Dakos **Barley rusk with tomatoes, cheese, olives and capers**

FROM **CRETE**

SERVES 1–2

1 large round barley rusk (approximately 10–12cm/ 4–5 inches in diameter, or use lightly toasted stale bread)
250g (9oz) ripe tomatoes or sweet cherry tomatoes
60ml (2fl oz) olive oil
1 teaspoon dried oregano
100g (3½oz) Cretan *mizithra, galomizithra, prentza* or feta (use feta if making the avocado twist)
1 tablespoon capers, drained, rinsed and dried
1–2 black olives
Salt and freshly ground black pepper

FOR THE AVOCADO TWIST
1 ripe avocado
1 tablespoon fresh lemon juice
1 tablespoon thinly sliced spring onions (scallions, optional)

Dakos, also known as *koukouvagia*, is my ultimate summer brunch-at-the-beach! Despite its closer resemblance to bruschetta, Greeks traditionally categorise it as a salad. Originating on Crete, this dish has gained widespread popularity throughout Greece. The classic recipe comprises simple ingredients: a barley rusk serves as the base, topped with freshly grated (shredded) or chopped tomatoes and their succulent juices, creamy white cheese or crumbled feta, oregano, a drizzle of olive oil, and is often garnished with olives or capers. Some regions substitute the rusks with stale bread, reminiscent of Kefalonia's *riganada* or similar Mediterranean dishes like the Italian *panzanella* or *frizella*, and the Spanish *pan con tomate*. If barley rusks aren't available, lightly toasted stale bread works just fine (it's also an excellent way to reduce food waste). Beyond the classic rendition, I enjoy incorporating mashed avocado, an ingredient that has become increasingly prominent in Crete over recent years.

If using a barley rusk, fill a bowl with water and soak the rusk for 4–5 seconds. Let it drain in a colander for 5 minutes and then place it on a serving plate. (If you only have small rusks, you can use a few more of these instead of the larger round one and follow the same method.)

If using stale bread, cut a slice about 3cm (1 inch) thick. Do not soak the bread; simply place it straight on a serving plate. (The bread will soften with the tomato juices.) If you don't have any stale bread, you can use lightly toasted fresh bread instead.

If making the avocado twist, scoop the flesh into a bowl and mash with a fork. Mix in the lemon juice and half of the crumbled feta. Season with salt and black pepper to taste.

Using the large holes of a box grater, grate (shred) the tomatoes into a bowl, reserving all the juices, until only the skins remain. Discard the skins. If using cherry tomatoes, blitz them in a food processor. Mix in half of the olive oil and half of the oregano, then season with salt to taste.

Pour the tomato mixture over the rusk or bread, then spoon or crumble the cheese on top. If making the avocado twist, spoon the avocado on top of the tomato, followed by the remaining feta.

Drizzle the remaining olive oil over the cheese, sprinkle the rest of the oregano on top, then garnish with the capers, olives and spring onions (if using). Serve immediately.

GREEK ISLAND HONEYS

Long before sugar, honey was highly valued as a sweetener. Every inhabited Greek island produces exceptional honey, capturing the essence of their landscape. This deep connection with an island's flora enhances the flavours, aromas and qualities of the honeys produced, offering health benefits from the plants and herbs they include. Some of the most famous varieties are harvested on the islands, including the driest regions, where thyme and other wildflower honeys are produced, such as the delicate lavender honey from Serifos. Thyme is prevalent in many honeys, whether in high percentage, such as the fantastic thyme honey of Kythera, or blended, such as the pine and thyme honey from Crete or the fir and thyme honey of Kefalonia. Several other varieties are produced, such as the creamy heather honey from Andros and Tinos, or the bitter Arbutus honey found on Ikaria, the Cretan carob honey, and the oak and wildflower honey from the mountains of Evia.

Honey is enjoyed in various ways throughout the islands, both in savoury and sweet recipes. It's a favourite for breakfast, drizzled over bread and butter or Greek-style doughnuts and pancakes like katimeria from Samos (see page 17) or Cretan cheese-stuffed pancakes (see page 15) and many other cheese pies. It pairs wonderfully with yogurt and fruit, and is commonly added to liqueurs, herbal teas and other beverages.

Greek desserts prominently feature honey, whether simply drizzled over treats like svingi (see page 192) or incorporated into syrups for cakes and sweets like baklava. Honey syrups feature in semolina and other cakes or cookies, such as the almond cookies from Kythira. On many islands, including Crete, they make xerotigana, festive, crispy fried pancakes that are drizzled with honey and sprinkled with ground walnuts or sesame seeds.

One of the most traditional treats featuring honey, found on nearly every island, are sesame bars known as pastelia. These bars are made with honey and sesame seeds and often cut into diamond shapes. On Tinos they are often left to dry on lemon or bitter orange leaves to absorb their aromatic essence. On Amorgos they add cumin seeds and on Rhodes where they call it melekouni, it's enriched with almonds, orange zest, cinnamon and clove, and traditionally offered at weddings, baptisms and other festive events.

On Sifnos, they make melopita (see page 186), a wonderful baked cheesecake with honey, and on Crete, locals heat up their local raki (grape distillate) with spices and mix it with honey to make rakomelo. On Zakynthos and Lefkada, they add honey in their mantolato (nougat) and on Ithaki they make rovani, a very sticky baked rice cake made with lots of honey.

Honey holds a cherished place in island culinary traditions, enriching both everyday meals and festive treats. It also mirrors the pristine nature and biodiversity of the Greek islands, embodying the essence of their unique landscapes and traditional practices.

ΜΕΛΙ
HONEY

Lychnarakia **Cheesecakes with cinnamon**

FROM **CRETE**

MAKES 30

FOR THE PASTRY
450–500g (15½–17½oz) plain (all-purpose) flour
2 teaspoons baking powder
Pinch of salt
1 teaspoon ground *mastiha* (optional, see tip below)
120g (4oz) strained Greek-style yogurt
150g (5½oz) granulated sugar
120g (4oz) butter, melted and cooled
1 large egg yolk, at room temperature
1 teaspoon vanilla extract
50ml (2fl oz) fresh orange juice (strained)

FOR THE FILLING
300g (10½oz) *mizithra* or ricotta, well drained and patted dry
100g (3½oz) caster (superfine) sugar
1 egg yolk, at room temperature
½ teaspoon orange zest (unwaxed)
½ teaspoon vanilla extract
Pinch of ground cinnamon
½ teaspoon ground *mastiha* (optional, see tip below)
1–2 tablespoons cornflour (corn starch, optional)

FOR BRUSHING
1 large egg yolk, mixed with 1 tablespoon water

Easter celebrations on the Greek islands bring forth an array of sweet or semi-sweet cakes and pies, crafted from the regional creamy cheeses that are abundant during springtime. Among these creations are magnificent offerings like the *melopita* from Sifnos and *patiniotiki* from Patmos, both resembling large cakes. Meanwhile, most Cycladic islands and Crete offer cupcake-sized cheesecakes resembling tarts, with either thick or thin pastry. Widely known as *tsibites*, which translates as 'pinched', these treats earn their name from the pinched pastry edges which ensure the cheese filling stays put and creates a charming pattern. Due to their widespread popularity, these delectable cheesecakes have transcended Easter festivities and are now enjoyed year-round on many islands. Personally, they rank among my favourite sweet treats from Greece and pair great with tea or coffee. You will find many equally delightful variations and names across the different islands; *melitinia*, *mizithropitakia*, *lychnarakia*, *melitera* or *kaltsounia*. Typically, the cheese filling is lightly sweetened with sugar and infused with flavours such as orange zest, *mastiha*, cinnamon and vanilla. Here, I offer a version from Crete, which has a slightly thicker pastry.

First, make the pastry. Combine the flour, baking powder, salt and *mastiha*, if using, in a bowl and set aside.

In the bowl of an electric stand mixer fitted with the whisk attachment, mix the yogurt and sugar until well combined. While mixing at medium speed, gradually pour in the cooled melted butter. Add the egg yolk and mix until fully incorporated. Next, add the vanilla extract and orange juice and mix well. The mixture should be creamy and smooth.

Switch to the hook attachment and, mixing at medium speed, gradually add enough flour to form a soft, smooth dough that is not sticky. Shape the dough into a ball, place it in a bowl, cover the bowl with cling film (plastic wrap) and let it rest in the fridge for 30 minutes while you prepare the filling.

Place the cheese in a fine sieve (strainer) to drain any excess liquid, then transfer it to a bowl. Using a fork or potato masher, thoroughly cream the cheese, then add the sugar and mix until well combined. Add in the egg yolk, orange zest, vanilla extract, cinnamon and *mastiha*, if using, then mix well. If the mixture feels too loose, incorporate the cornflour. (If you are preparing the filling ahead of time, cover the bowl and chill in the fridge until needed.)

Preheat the oven to 170°C/150°C fan/325°F/gas 3. Line two baking trays with parchment paper.

Recipe continues overleaf

Divide the dough into 3 or 4 equal pieces and roll each one into a ball. On a lightly floured work surface, roll out the first ball into a sheet, about 4mm (⅛ inch) thick. Using an 8cm (3 inch) cookie cutter, cut out disks. Spoon a heaped teaspoon of filling into the centre of each pastry disk, then use one of the three methods below to shape the cheesecakes:

For the crimping method: Crimp the edges of the pastry by hand using a deep pinching action all around and towards the centre to create small pleats and shape them into tartlets.

For the folding method: Fold each side of the pastry slightly over the filling to form a triangle, leaving a small part of the filling uncovered in the centre.

Using tart molds: Small tart molds can be used for ease, if preferred.

Place each cheesecake on the prepared baking tray, leaving a small gap between each one. Repeat the same process with the remaining dough and filling.

Whisk the egg yolk with the water and gently brush each cheesecake. Bake in the hot oven for 25–30 minutes, or until golden. Remove from the oven, cover with a clean dish towel and let them cool completely.

When stored in a cool, dark place, these cheesecakes will keep for up to 4–5 days. If it is particularly hot or humid (and you plan to store them for more than a couple of days), I recommend storing them in an airtight container in the fridge. Before serving, allow them to come to room temperature for the best taste and texture.

TIP

When grinding *mastiha*, it's best to freeze it beforehand. Once sufficiently chilled, use a pestle and mortar along with a pinch of sugar to break it down into a fine powder.

Paximadakia **Twice-baked olive oil cookies with orange and aniseed**

FROM **TINOS**

MAKES 25

430g (15oz) plain (all-purpose) flour
1 teaspoon baking powder
¾ teaspoon ground aniseed
130ml (41½fl oz) olive oil
100g (3½oz) caster (superfine) sugar
Zest of 1 orange (unwaxed)
1 teaspoon bicarbonate of soda (baking soda)
80ml (2½fl oz) orange juice (see tip below)

Greeks love to bake. There are hundreds of recipes for cookies, both sweet and savoury, prepared on the islands. When you visit, you must go to a traditional bakery to experience the abundance of locally baked goodies. This is one of my favourites: a twice-baked olive oil cookie that is slightly sweet and pairs well with tea or coffee. On some islands, currants, almonds or other nuts are added, or they're spiced up with cinnamon and cloves. My favourite version includes orange and a touch of aniseed, as they typically do on Tinos. In traditional cafés on that island, these cookies are offered complimentary with every coffee order. Each time I eat one, I am transported to the lovely Kafe-nai café in the stunning village of Volax, where poems are written on the doors and windows. They're really easy to make, low in sugar and vegan. I usually keep these cookies simple, but every now and then I like to roll them in sesame seeds before baking. If you fancy a bit of variety, you could coat them in other seeds, such as nigella or poppy seeds, or add chopped nuts or dried fruit to the dough.

In a bowl, combine the flour with the baking powder and ground aniseed. Set aside.

In a separate bowl or the bowl of an electric stand mixer, whisk the olive oil with the sugar and orange zest for a few minutes until well combined.

In a large glass or jug (pitcher), stir the bicarbonate of soda into the orange juice (it will rise and froth, so be careful not to spill it). Add the orange juice to the olive oil mixture. Mix well to combine.

Gradually add the flour while mixing either with a silicone spatula (and later kneading by hand) or at medium-low speed with the paddle attachment, until all is incorporated. The dough should not be kneaded too much. It should be smooth, soft, and slightly oily without being too sticky. If it's too sticky, add a bit of extra flour, but no more than a couple of tablespoons.

Shape the dough into a ball, place it in a bowl, cover with a clean cloth and let it rest at room temperature for 15–20 minutes.

Preheat the oven to 180°C/160°C fan/350°F/gas 4. Line a baking tray with parchment paper.

Divide the dough into two equal pieces and shape each into a log about 3–4cm (1–1½ inches) in diameter. Place them on the baking tray, leaving a small gap between each one, and gently press down to slightly flatten them. Using a sharp knife, score slightly diagonal slices about 1cm (⅓ inch) wide, cutting halfway through the dough.

Recipe continues overleaf

Bake in the hot oven for 25 minutes or until golden. Remove the cookies from the oven, turn the oven off and let them cool for 15 minutes.

Once the cookies have cooled down a bit, carefully slice them all the way through and lay the sliced cookies flat and side by side on the same tray. Turn the oven on again (it should still be hot) and set the temperature to 160°C/140°C fan/300°F/gas 2.

Return the cookies to the oven and bake for a further 15–20 minutes or until they turn dark golden (on their cut sides) and harden. Remove from the oven and let cool completely.

When stored in an airtight container, these cookies can be kept for up to 2 weeks.

TIP

After you have zested the orange, squeeze the fresh juice from the fruit. An orange contains on average 70ml (2fl oz) of juice, so if necessary, add enough water to make it up to 80ml (2½fl oz).

MINI

Small Plates to Share

CHAPTER 2

Maintanosalata **Parsley dip**

FROM **SYROS**

SERVES 6–8

200g (7oz) stale bread (without crusts)
60g (2oz) parsley leaves
1–2 garlic cloves, peeled and roughly chopped
3 tablespoons fresh lemon juice (or to taste)
70ml (5 tablespoons) olive oil
30g (1oz) capers, drained, rinsed, dried and finely chopped
Salt and freshly ground black pepper

This parsley dip hails from Syros, the capital of the Cycladic islands. Despite its small size, the island's main town, Ermoupoli, which is named after Hermes, boasts a unique noble flair, evident in both its architecture and cuisine. This versatile, bright green dip enhances a variety of dishes. I love it served with fried fish (do try it with classic fish and chips) or calamari. It also pairs great with raw, grilled or fried vegetables and grilled meats, plus you can use it in sandwiches. The dip can be stored in the fridge for a few days, making it a convenient and flavourful addition to any meal. If you aren't a big fan of garlic, you can reduce the amount or omit it altogether.

Soak the bread in just enough water to soften it. Drain very well and let it stand in a colander to dry. Crumble the bread into a bowl.

Pat the parsley leaves with paper towels to make sure they are dry, then place in a food processor along with the garlic, lemon juice and a little salt. Blitz the parsley to a coarse paste.

Add the crumbled bread to the food processor and blitz again until smooth. While blending, pour in the oil, a little at a time, until it is all incorporated. The dip should be smooth and creamy. Stir in the chopped capers, season with salt and freshly ground black pepper to taste and mix well. Drizzle with a little extra olive oil before serving. Transfer the dip to a sterilised jar. When stored in the fridge, this dip can be kept for up to 3 days.

Prentza **Creamed feta and herb dip**

FROM **KEFALONIA**

SERVES 6–8

200g (7oz) feta
200g (7oz) fresh *mizithra*, *anthotiro* or ricotta
1 teaspoon dried marjoram
¾ teaspoon dried *thymbra* (wild thyme) or thyme
1 hot green chilli/chile, finely chopped (optional)
90ml (6 tablespoons) olive oil
Freshly ground black pepper

Prentza is a cheese by-product prepared in Kefalonia and other Ionian islands. It is made from leftover crumbled feta and the *mizithra* that settles at the bottom of aging barrels. To prevent waste, the cheeses are collected and mixed with olive oil, *thymbra* (wild thyme) and oregano or wild marjoram, known locally as *sapsycho*, which is a staple herb in Ionian island cuisine. This mixture produces a deliciously creamy cheese that can be served as a dip or used in salads, on bruschetta or as part of a cheese platter. Sometimes I like to make it spicy by adding some chopped green chillies to the mix.

Crumble the feta into a bowl and add the other cheese. Thoroughly blend the two together until smooth. Mix in the dried herbs and chopped chilli, if using, ensuring they are well combined. While stirring vigorously, slowly add the olive oil. Season with black pepper to taste. Transfer the dip to a sterilised jar. When stored in the fridge, this dip can be kept for up to 2 weeks.

Taramosalata **Classic taramosalata with olive oil and lemon**

FROM **LESVOS**

SERVES 6–8

100–150g (3½–5oz) melba toasts (depending on how thick you like the dip)
50g (1¾oz) white fish roe
3–4 tablespoons fresh lemon juice, plus extra to taste
1 small onion, peeled and roughly chopped
60ml (2fl oz) olive oil
60ml (2fl oz) sunflower oil
1 tablespoon chopped dill (optional)
Extra virgin olive oil, to drizzle (optional)
Olives, to garnish

An all-time favourite dip to enjoy with bread, raw vegetables or French fries. It also goes great with grilled seafood, such as calamari or octopus. There are two common ways to make taramosalata: by using a mortar and pestle for an old-school, chunky dip or by making it in a food processor for a creamier texture. It can be made with bread, rusks or melba toasts, or even with boiled potatoes. Remember to source a good-quality fish roe, which should have a creamy beige colour rather than red or pink.

Fill a bowl with cold water. Dip the melba toasts in the water for 6–8 seconds to slightly moisten them, then place in a fine sieve (strainer) and leave to drain well. (Don't soak the melba toasts for too long as they become very mushy and make the taramosalata less thick.)

Spoon the fish roe and lemon juice into a blender and briefly pulse. (This releases the flavours of the fish roe.) Add the chopped onion and pulse again. Add the well-drained melba toasts and blend until smooth. While blending, gradually add both oils, little by little, to achieve a velvety, smooth and thick texture. If you prefer it less thick, you can thin down the taramosalata with a little cold water. If you like it thicker, add an extra melba toast.

Stir in the chopped dill, if using, and some extra lemon juice to taste. Spoon the taramosalata into an airtight container with a lid and place in the fridge for at least 30 minutes before serving.

When stored in an airtight container in the fridge, this taramosalata can be kept for up to 6 days.

Shown on page 35.

Tzatziki **Tzatziki four ways**

FROM **THE ISLANDS**

Tzatziki needs no introduction; it's a well-loved classic that pairs wonderfully with many dishes. The key to a great tzatziki is high-quality yogurt: it should be well-strained, thick and creamy. While the classic version includes cucumber, tzatziki can be made with various ingredients to suit your taste. Choose your favourite variation and always serve it chilled!

Classic tzatziki with cucumber and dill

SERVES 6–8

- 400g (14oz) strained Greek-style yogurt
- 1 large cucumber, deseeded (no need to peel)
- 3–4 garlic cloves, peeled and minced
- 2–3 tablespoons white wine vinegar
- 90ml (6 tablespoons) extra virgin olive oil, plus extra to serve
- 1 tablespoon chopped dill
- Salt and freshly ground black pepper

Spoon the yogurt into a fine sieve (strainer) to remove any excess water.

Using the large holes of a box grater, grate (shred) the cucumber into a colander. Sprinkle over a little salt to draw the water out of the cucumber, then let it stand for 10–15 minutes.

Once drained, squeeze the grated cucumber with your hands to remove any excess water. (Don't throw this cucumber water away – it's a great addition to a gin and tonic.)

Spoon the yogurt into a large mixing bowl and stir in the cucumber, garlic and vinegar. While stirring vigorously, gradually add the olive oil. Season the tzatziki with salt and black pepper to taste, then mix in the chopped dill. Cover and chill in the fridge until ready to serve.

Serve the tzatziki drizzled with a little extra virgin olive oil, if you like.

Tzatziki with capers

SERVES 6–8

- All of the ingredients for the Classic Tzatziki (see above)
- 1 tablespoon chopped capers, plus a few whole capers to finish

Follow the instructions for the Classic Tzatziki. Before serving, stir in the chopped capers along with the dill.

Serve the tzatziki drizzled with a little extra virgin olive oil and a few whole capers scattered on top.

Shown on page 39.

Tzatziki with beetroot and carrot

SERVES 4–6

- 300g (10½oz) strained Greek-style yogurt
- 2 small beetroot (beets), peeled and grated (shredded)
- 1 carrot, peeled and grated (shredded)
- 2 garlic cloves, peeled and minced
- 3 tablespoons cider vinegar
- 3 tablespoons extra virgin olive oil, plus extra to serve
- 2 tablespoons finely chopped dill
- ½ teaspoon grated (shredded) orange zest (unwaxed)
- Salt and freshly ground black pepper
- Toasted sesame seeds, to serve

Spoon the yogurt into a fine sieve (strainer) to remove any excess water.

Place the grated (shredded) beetroot in a colander. Sprinkle over a little salt, then let stand for 10 minutes.

Spoon the yogurt into a large mixing bowl and stir in the beetroot, carrot, garlic and vinegar. While stirring vigorously, gradually add the olive oil. Season the tzatziki with salt and black pepper to taste, then mix in the chopped dill and orange zest. Cover and chill in the fridge until ready to serve.

Serve the tzatziki drizzled with a little extra virgin olive oil and sprinkled with toasted sesame seeds, if you like.

Tzatziki with avocado and mint

SERVES 4–6

- 200g (7oz) strained Greek-style yogurt
- 2 tablespoons grated (shredded) cucumber
- 1 ripe avocado
- 3 tablespoons fresh lemon juice
- 2 garlic cloves, peeled and minced (optional)
- 1 tablespoon extra virgin olive oil, plus extra to serve
- 1 teaspoon ground cumin, plus extra to serve
- 2 tablespoons finely chopped mint
- 1 teaspoon grated (shredded) lemon zest (unwaxed)
- Salt and freshly ground black pepper

Spoon the yogurt into a fine sieve (strainer) to remove any excess water.

Place the grated (shredded) cucumber in a colander. Sprinkle over a little salt to draw the water out of the cucumber, then let stand for 10–15 minutes.

Once drained, squeeze the grated cucumber with your hands to remove any excess water.

In a separate bowl or in a food processor, cream the avocado with the lemon juice until smooth. Mix the avocado into the yogurt, followed by the cucumber and garlic. While stirring vigorously, gradually add the olive oil. Stir in the ground cumin and season with salt and black pepper to taste, then mix in the mint and lemon zest. Cover and chill in the fridge until ready to serve.

Serve the tzatziki drizzled with a little extra virgin olive oil, if you like.

Fava **Creamed yellow split peas**

FROM **SANTORINI**

SERVES 6-8

- 500g (18oz) Greek yellow split peas (available from specialist stores and online)
- 6 tablespoons olive oil, plus extra to serve
- 1 large onion, chopped
- 1 bay leaf
- 1 thyme sprig
- 1.5 litres (50fl oz) hot vegetable stock or water
- Juice of ½ lemon (or more to taste)
- Salt and freshly ground black pepper

TO SERVE

- Olive oil
- Lemon juice
- Thinly sliced or finely chopped onion
- Finely chopped parsley
- Capers (optional)

This is the simplest and most classic way to prepare Greek fava, a traditional creamy dish made from the various types of yellow split peas that thrive on specific islands with Santorini's *lathouri* standing out. Fava is a staple on every restaurant menu. Its creamy, mild flavour makes it incredibly versatile, pairing well with many different foods. I particularly enjoy it with fish or seafood, but it's also delightful warm as a main dish with some salad or boiled veggies and greens with good bread on the side.

Historically, islanders have had to be inventive and resourceful with the limited ingredients available, making traditional cuisine all about creativity and minimising food waste. Leftover fava that has thickened in the fridge is transformed into delicious zero-waste fritters – see the recipe opposite.

Rinse the split peas thoroughly under cold running water, transfer them to a bowl, cover with fresh water and leave to soak for 20 minutes. (This improves the final texture.) Drain the split peas in a colander and set aside.

Place a heavy-based pot with a lid over a medium heat and add 2 tablespoons of the olive oil. Once hot, add the onion, bay leaf and thyme and sauté until the onion has softened. Add the split peas, followed by the stock or water, and set the heat to medium-high heat. When it begins to boil, reduce the heat to low and skim off any foam using a slotted spoon. Keep the heat low, leave the lid of the pot ajar, and avoid stirring while it cooks. Gently simmer for 50–60 minutes or until the fava turns creamy.

Remove and discard the bay leaf and thyme sprig, then season with salt and stir the fava with a wooden spoon or silicone spatula. It should have a creamy consistency, like a thick soup. If not, let it simmer a few minutes longer. Remove the pan from heat, mix in the lemon juice and the remaining olive oil. Using a handheld stick (immersion) blender, blitz the fava until smooth. Taste and adjust the seasoning, if necessary.

Fava can be served warm or at room temperature, however it will thicken further as it cools. When reheating, add a little broth or water to thin it down.

To serve, spoon onto a plate and drizzle with more olive oil and lemon juice to taste. (Greeks often squeeze the juice of half a lemon on a portion.) Mix well to combine. Top with thinly sliced or finely chopped raw onion, finely chopped parsley and scatter some capers on top for extra flavour, if you like.

Fava fritters

FROM **SANTORINI**

MAKES 25–30

- 600g (1lb 5oz) leftover cooked yellow fava (see opposite, chilled in the fridge)
- 4 spring onions (scallions), chopped (green part too)
- 6–7 sun-dried tomatoes, chopped (about 40g/1½oz)
- 2 tablespoons chopped capers
- 3–4 tablespoons finely chopped parsley
- ½ teaspoon dried oregano
- 50g (1¾oz) cornmeal, plus extra for coating the fritters
- 1 tablespoon olive oil
- 1 tablespoon ground flaxseed
- Salt and freshly ground black pepper
- Sunflower oil, for frying

It's always best to make these fritters with leftover fava that has chilled in the fridge for at least a few hours and thickened well. If you have made the fava intentionally to prepare the fritters, let it cool down completely for at least 3–4 hours before you follow the instructions below. I keep them vegan and gluten-free, adding sun-dried tomatoes and capers for texture and flavour. While these fritters can also be baked (or air-fried), I prefer them shallow fried because they turn crispier on the outside while remaining creamy inside. This is an excellent choice for those following a plant-based diet, as Greek yellow split peas are a very good source of protein.

Put the thickened fava in a large mixing bowl. Add the spring onions, sun-dried tomatoes, capers, parsley and oregano to the bowl and mix well with a silicone spatula, gradually adding the cornmeal while mixing. You may need to adjust the amount of cornmeal depending on the consistency of the leftover fava – you must be able to shape the mixture into balls without it being too thick. Cover the fava with a clean dish towel and place it in the fridge for 30 minutes. Once chilled, shape the fava into small balls, roughly the size of a walnut. Lightly press each ball to flatten them a little into a patty, but not too much or they will fall apart during cooking. Spread some cornmeal over a tray and use it to coat each patty.

To fry the fritters, place a large, deep frying pan (skillet) over a medium-high heat. Pour enough oil into the pan to reach a depth of 2cm (¾ inch) and let it heat up. Once hot, carefully lower the fritters into the oil – only add a few at a time to maintain the oil temperature and ensure they turn crispy. Fry the fritters on each side for 2–3 minutes or until crisp and golden brown. Once cooked, transfer the fritters to a plate lined with paper towels to absorb any excess oil.

To bake the fritters, preheat the oven to 200°C/180°C fan/400°F/gas 6 and line a large baking tray with parchment paper. Arrange the patties on the tray and bake in the hot oven for 10–15 minutes or until golden. Using a spatula, carefully flip the fritters over and bake for a further 5–10 minutes or until golden on both sides.

ISLAND GOATS AND PIGS

Pork and goat meat are both essential to traditional Greek island cuisine, deeply intertwined with the local culture and history. A familiar sight across the islands, goats are exceptional climbers and foragers, thriving even on remote, rugged terrain. Their diverse diet of wild shrubs, herbs and figs results in lean meat and flavourful milk, in which you can also detect the salty island air and occasional sea water they drink.

Goats' milk is integral to producing cheeses, yogurt, butter and the renowned Cretan specialty, staka. This traditional dairy delight, made from the cream of goats' or ewes' milk and thickened with flour, imparts a luxurious, buttery flavour to dishes like fried eggs. Preservation techniques for goats' milk also includes rustic local pasta recipes, such as trahanas and xinohontro.

Goat meat holds a revered place in traditional island fare, particularly on islands where it is more readily available than lamb or mutton. The meat is used in roasts, stews and festive dishes, such as patatato from Amorgos (see page 89), or prepared as an Easter favourite, such as vyzanti from Karpathos, mououri from Kalymnos and lambriatis from Andros. Often the meat is sealed in locally crafted ceramic pots and cooked overnight in wood-burning ovens.

Pork is equally significant, particularly through the custom of choirosfagia, a traditional pig-slaughtering practice that is carried out even today on several islands. Even the poorest households would traditionally raise a pig to meet their yearly meat needs, feeding it acorns, nettles and dried figs - which are said to impart a sweeter taste to the liver. This timing takes advantage of the cooler weather to preserve the meat and produce items like sausages, siglino (pork preserved in olive oil), and other delicacies, such as the Cycladic louza (pork cured in salt and marinated in red wine, herbs and spices and finally air-dried) or the Cretan apaki (pork tenderloin cured in vinegar and then smoked with local herbs such as oregano and rosemary). From the head, brawn is prepared, known as pichti or tsiladia and the fat with some meat attached is also fried and this snack is known as tsigarides, which was often served on bread to workers in the fields and olive groves. The pig's skin was shaved and then dried and preserved and they used it as a flavour enhancer in several humble, plant-based dishes such as beans. The best cuts of pork were reserved for the Christmas and other festivities, with typical recipes including roasts, stews with celery or cabbage, and the traditional lachanodolmades (meat-stuffed cabbage rolls, see page 90). Every single part of the pig is utilised, reflecting the resourcefulness and practicality of rural island life.

Both animals are central to island life, providing sustenance year-round while also playing a key role in local traditions. Goats and pigs alike symbolise the resourcefulness of island life, with their meat and dairy products woven into the rich culinary traditions of Greece's islands.

Salatouri **Boiled fish with herbs and capers**

FROM **PAROS**

SERVES 4–6

FOR THE FISH
1kg (2lb 4oz) whole turbot (either 1 large or 2 small fish), gutted and descaled
1 onion, peeled and quartered
1 garlic clove, peeled and minced
2 bay leaves
1 thyme sprig
3–4 whole allspice berries
4–5 whole black peppercorns
1 teaspoon olive oil
Salt

FOR THE DRESSING
2 heaped teaspoons Dijon mustard
90ml (3fl oz) fresh lemon juice
180ml (6fl oz) olive oil
½ teaspoon lemon zest (unwaxed)
Salt and freshly ground black pepper

TO SERVE
1 small red onion, peeled and chopped
5 tablespoons finely chopped parsley
3 tablespoons finely chopped dill
50g (1¾oz) capers, drained, rinsed and dried
Freshly ground black pepper

This wonderful dish reminds me of carefree childhood summers on Paros, where my grandfather George came from. At the picturesque port of Aliki, dozens of tables are lined up by the water, just a few metres away from the moored fishing boats. Octopuses and butterflied mackerels (locals call them *gouna*, which translates as fur) hang on ropes to sun-dry and the smell of charcoal-grilled seafood wafts on the breeze. The best time to be there is before sunset when the sky starts to turn pink, purple and orange. You order a glass of *suma* (local grappa) and a plate of *salatouri*, the local specialty. This light, cold fish dish is all I crave to eat whenever I'm on Paros.

The fish traditionally used is either skate or turbot, but other options are Pacific halibut, Dover sole, flounder, tilapia or Pacific cod. If a whole fish is not available, this can also be made with filleted fish, although it's tastier to boil it whole. A similar dish is also prepared on other Cycladic islands and on Kalymnos, where they call it *karkani*.

Fill a large saucepan with water and add the onion, garlic, bay leaves, thyme, allspice berries, peppercorns and a pinch of salt. Place the pan over a medium heat and bring the water to a slow boil. Once boiling, submerge the fish in the water. Add the olive oil to the water, then gently boil the fish for 15–20 minutes or until the flesh is opaque and flakes easily with a fork. Remove the pan from the heat and transfer the fish to a plate to cool. (Reserve the fish stock for another use – a comforting soup with rice or vegetables, or for a risotto.)

Once the fish has cooled slightly, remove the skin and bones. Using a paring knife, make a small incision at the tail end to get a grip on the skin. Gently lift the skin at the incision or edge using your fingers or knife. Working slowly, carefully peel the skin away from the flesh. The skin should come off relatively easily if the fish is properly cooked. Lift the flesh off the central bone, check and remove any small bones using fish tweezers, then flake the meat into a bowl. (You should have around 450g/1lb of meat.) Cover the bowl and place in the fridge to chill.

Meanwhile, make the dressing. Spoon the mustard into a bowl, then mix in the lemon juice. Gradually whisk in the olive oil until everything is well combined and smooth. Stir in the lemon zest and season with salt and black pepper to taste.

When ready to serve, remove the chilled fish from the fridge. Add the red onion to the bowl with the fish, pour over the dressing and mix well. Stir in the parsley, dill and capers, then add a little freshly ground black pepper, if you like. Transfer to a serving plate and enjoy cold.

Kolokithokeftedes **Spring courgette fritters**

FROM **THASOS**

MAKES 25–30

400g (14oz) courgettes (zucchini)
100g (3½oz) courgette (zucchini) flowers (or use greens such as spinach, sorrel and collard greens), roughly chopped
100g (3½oz) flour (or cornmeal to make it gluten-free)
½ teaspoon baking powder
6 spring onions (scallions), chopped (green part too)
3 tablespoons chopped parsley
3 tablespoons chopped mint
90g (3oz) feta, crumbled
60g (2oz) *kefalotyri* or pecorino cheese, grated (shredded)
2 eggs, beaten
Salt and freshly ground black pepper
Cornmeal, to coat the fritters
Sunflower oil, to fry (optional)

TO SERVE

Tzatziki (see page 37) or plain yogurt

Courgette (zucchini) fritters are one of the classic dishes prepared on every single island during summer when courgettes are abundant. In Greece, it is common to buy courgettes with their delicate flowers still attached. On some islands, like Thasos in northern Aegean or Crete, they include the flowers in the courgette fritter mixture. Other greens can be added too – local recipes call for foraged seasonal greens, but spinach, sorrel and collard greens all work perfectly. Fresh herbs and spring onions (scallions) are essential components, imparting both texture and flavour. The patties may be fried, which is the custom, but they are also wonderful when baked or air-fried.

Using the large holes of a box grater, grate (shred) the courgettes into a bowl, add ¾ teaspoon salt and mix well to combine. Place the courgettes in a fine sieve (strainer) and leave to drain for 20 minutes. Repeat this with the courgette flowers or greens, if using, adding ¼ teaspoon salt. Squeeze the courgettes and greens to remove any excess moisture and transfer to a large mixing bowl. (You don't need to do this with the courgette flowers.) Add the spring onions, parsley, mint and cheeses, season with black pepper and gently mix until just combined.

In a separate bowl, combine the flour and baking powder. Incorporate the beaten eggs into the courgette mixture, then while stirring, gradually add the flour and baking powder until the mixture is firm enough to shape into a patty – if not, add a little more flour. Cover the bowl with cling film (plastic wrap) and chill in the fridge for 30–60 minutes. (This step is optional, but chilling the mixture makes it easier to form it into patties and enhances the flavours.)

Once chilled, shape the courgette mixture into balls, roughly the size of a walnut, then lightly press each one to flatten them a little into a patty. Spread some cornmeal over a tray and use it to coat each patty.

To fry the fritters, place a large, deep frying pan (skillet) over a medium-high heat. Pour in enough oil to reach a depth of 2cm (¾ inch). Working in small batches, lower the fritters into the hot oil and fry for 2–3 minutes on each side or until golden and crisp. Transfer to a plate lined with paper towels to absorb any excess oil.

To bake the fritters, preheat the oven to 200°C/180°C fan/400°F/gas 6 and line a large baking tray with parchment paper. Arrange the patties on the tray and bake in the hot oven for 25–30 minutes, or until golden. For extra crispy fritters, flip them over half way through the cooking time.

Serve the courgette fritters with some tzatziki or plain yogurt on the side.

Pitia with skordalia **Chickpea balls with an almond and garlic dipping sauce**

FROM **NISYROS**

MAKES 35–40

FOR THE CHICKPEA BALLS
250g (9oz) dried chickpeas (garbanzo beans)
70g (2½oz) grated (shredded) pumpkin, butternut squash or carrot
1 small onion, finely chopped
1 garlic clove, peeled and minced
1 small tomato (around 80g), chopped
3 tablespoons chopped mint
2 tablespoons chopped parsley
2 tablespoons chopped dill
1 teaspoon dried oregano
1 teaspoon salt
½ teaspoon freshly ground black pepper
150g (5½oz) self-raising flour
1 teaspoon olive oil
Sunflower oil, for frying

FOR THE SKORDALIA
150g (5½oz) stale bread
50g (1¾oz) blanched untoasted almonds
2–3 small garlic cloves, peeled and roughly chopped
1 tablespoon white wine vinegar
1 tablespoon fresh lemon juice
100ml (3½fl oz) olive oil
¼ teaspoon lemon zest (unwaxed)
Salt and freshly ground black pepper

A common way of using chickpeas (garbanzo beans) on the islands is to shape them into balls that are then shallow fried; they are similar to falafels but a little lighter and with more herbs. I like to use dried chickpeas, because they make for crispy fritters, but bear in mind they will need to be soaked for 24 hours first. Several variations of this recipe can be found across the different islands, like on Sifnos where they mush boiled potatoes into the mix, or on Kastelorizo where they use ground cumin and oregano. On the volcanic island of Nisyros, chickpea balls are especially popular served with their traditional *skordalia*, a dipping sauce made with almonds and garlic. Almond trees are abundant on Nisyros, where they are celebrated with an annual festival in August dedicated to their local *soumada* (almond drink).

A day ahead, place the dried chickpeas in a large bowl and cover with plenty of water. Leave them to soak for 24 hours.

To make the *skordalia*, soak the bread in enough water to soften it, then crumble into a fine sieve (strainer) and remove any water by pressing against the sieve. Place the almonds and garlic in a food processor and pulse until finely ground. Gradually add the soaked bread and pulse until a smooth paste forms. Add the vinegar and lemon juice, them pulse again. While processing, gradually add the olive oil until fully incorporated. Season with salt and black pepper, then mix in the lemon zest. Cover and chill in the fridge until ready to serve.

Check the chickpeas have softened. They will feel crispy, like a nut, but you should be able to bite into them. Drain the chickpeas in a colander and set aside to dry. Working in batches, place the softened chickpeas in a food processor and pulse until coarsely chopped – don't overprocess, leaving them slightly chunky is preferable – then tip into a large bowl. Add the pumpkin, squash or carrot along with the onion, garlic, tomato, herbs and oregano. Season with salt and black pepper. Knead well to combine, while gradually adding in the flour until it's all incorporated. The mixture should be firm enough to form a ball – if not, add more flour. Shape the mixture into small balls, each weighing about 40g (1½oz).

Place a large frying pan (skillet) over a medium-high heat. Pour enough oil into the pan to reach a depth of 2cm (¾ inch). Once hot, lower the chickpea balls into the oil – add a few at a time to maintain the oil temperature and ensure they turn crispy. Fry the balls for 2–3 minutes or until golden and crispy. Turn the balls over and fry for a further 1–2 minutes or until golden and crisp on all sides. Transfer the balls to a plate lined with paper towels to absorb any excess oil.

Serve the chickpea balls with the *skordalia*.

Keftedakia **Grilled or fried meatballs with mint**

FROM **FOLEGANDROS**

MAKES 10–12 GRILLED MEATBALLS OR 35 FRIED MEATBALLS

160g (5½oz) stale bread (without crusts)
350g (12½oz) finely minced (ground) beef
350g (12½oz) finely minced (ground) pork
1 onion, peeled and grated (shredded) or finely chopped
1 heaped teaspoon tomato paste (concentrated purée)
1 tablespoon red wine vinegar
1 tablespoon olive oil
¼ teaspoon dried oregano
1 teaspoon dried mint
3–4 tablespoons chopped mint leaves, plus 2 tablespoons finely chopped mint leaves
3–4 tablespoons chopped parsley, plus 1 tablespoon finely chopped parsley
¾–1 teaspoon salt
½ teaspoon freshly ground black pepper
1 large egg, beaten
Flour, for coating the meatballs (if frying)
Sunflower oil, for frying or olive oil, for grilling

The classic meatballs found on every island are delightful, featuring lots of chopped fresh mint. Typically made with a mix of minced (ground) pork and beef, the meatballs can either be grilled or fried (including in an air fryer). Most simple tavernas around the islands serve these fried, and they are usually delightfully crispy and flavourful, thanks to the herbs. Boukla, the old taverna in Folegandros, has famously been preparing them this way for decades. They are often served as a meze to share or as a main dish, usually accompanied by fried potatoes, Greek salad and tzatziki. These meatballs make a great snack and can even be enjoyed cold. They are easy to pack and transport, making them ideal for picnics and lunchboxes. Additionally, they can be added to sandwiches or wraps or they can be mixed into a tomato sauce to serve with pasta, rice or mashed potatoes.

Soak the bread in just enough water to soften it. Drain very well and let it stand in a colander to dry.

Place the beef and pork mince in a large mixing bowl. Add the chopped onion, tomato paste, vinegar, olive oil, dried and fresh herbs. Season with the salt and freshly ground black pepper. Add the beaten egg and crumble in the soaked bread. Knead the mixture until well combined. Cover the bowl and place in the fridge to rest for 20–30 minutes or longer if you have time.

If frying the meatballs, shape the mixture into small balls, roughly the size of a ping pong ball. Place a large, deep frying pan (skillet) over a medium-high heat. Pour enough oil into the pan to fry the meatballs and let it heat up. Spread some flour over shallow tray and roll the meatballs in the flour. Tap each one to remove any excess flour. Once the oil is hot, working in batches, carefully lower in the first meatballs – only add around ten at a time to maintain the oil temperature and ensure they turn crispy. Fry the meatballs for about 6 minutes, turning them frequently, until lightly browned. Once cooked, transfer the meatballs to a plate lined with paper towels to absorb any excess oil. (The meatballs can also be cooked in an air fryer.)

If grilling the meatballs, shape the mixture into round or oblong patties, each weighing about 100g (3½oz). Cook them in a well-heat, cast-iron griddle pan on a preheated barbecue for 5–6 minutes on each side. The cooking time may vary, depending on your preferred level of doneness.

Fish & Seafood

CHAPTER 3

Midia ahnista me ouzo **Steamed mussels with ouzo and fennel**

FROM **LESVOS**

SERVES 4

- 1kg (2lb 4oz) fresh live mussels
- 60g (2oz) butter
- 1 fennel bulb, trimmed, halved and thinly sliced (reserve any fronds to serve)
- 4–5 spring onions (scallions), thinly sliced
- 3–4 garlic cloves, peeled and thinly sliced
- 2 bay leaves
- 100ml (3½fl oz) ouzo
- 3–4 small thyme sprigs
- Zest of 1 small lemon
- 3–4 tablespoons chopped parsley
- Freshly ground black pepper

Nestled in the southern part of Lesvos, the Gulf of Kalloni is an almost entirely enclosed, tranquil body of water, like a big lake, with a narrow opening to the Aegean Sea. This serene gulf is embraced by rolling hills and gentle mountains, painting a picturesque landscape with a unique microclimate. Celebrated for its rich biodiversity, the gulf is a haven for numerous species of birds, fish and other varieties of seafood, some of which are unique in Greece. It's particularly renowned for its sardines, known as *papalina*.

Mussel farming thrives in Lesvos. When in season, the much-anticipated *havara* (wild mussels) are harvested by locals. These mussels are prepared in a myriad of delightful ways – paired with feta and tomatoes, and served with rice, orzo or other pasta. One of my most cherished recipes is *ahnista* (steamed mussels), which is a light and satisfying way to enjoy them. I love cooking mussels with ouzo, another beloved product of Lesvos, creating a dish that is bursting with flavour and lovely aromas.

Wash the mussels to remove any dirt or grit. If any mussels are open, tap them on the counter – if they close, they are alive; if they remain open, discard them.

Place a large, shallow pot or deep pan with a well-fitting lid over a medium heat. Add half the butter to the pot and, once hot, add the sliced fennel bulb, spring onions, garlic and bay leaves. Cook until the vegetables start to soften.

Pour the ouzo into the pot and add the remaining butter. When everything starts to simmer, add the mussels and thyme sprigs. Immediately cover the pot and let the mussels simmer for 2 minutes. Without removing the lid, shake the pot to move the mussels around. Let them cook for a further 1 minute before repeating this process (the total cooking time should be about 6 minutes).

Take off the lid and mix the mussels well in the cooking liquid in the pan. Check to make sure that all the mussels have opened. Discard any unopened mussels. Add the lemon zest, parsley and plenty of black pepper, then cover the pot and shake again.

Transfer the mussels to a deep serving platter and spoon over the sauce along with the cooked fennel and spring onions. Scatter over any roughly chopped fennel fronds, if using. Serve the mussels with warm hunks of toasted bread.

Psarosoupa **Easy fish soup with egg and lemon sauce**

FROM **PAROS**

SERVES 4

1 whole pollock (around 800g/1lb 12oz), scaled and cleaned
½ lemon
1 onion, peeled and quartered
4–5 leaf celery stalks
1 tomato, peeled, quartered and deseeded
3–4 whole black peppercorns
2 allspice berries (optional)
2 carrots, cut into 2cm (⅔ inch) thick slices
2 potatoes, peeled and quartered
2 small courgettes (zucchini, about 200g/7oz), cut into 2cm (⅔ inch) thick slices
80g (2½oz) short or medium-grained white rice
Salt and freshly ground black pepper

FOR THE SAUCE
2 eggs
4 tablespoons fresh lemon juice

TO SERVE
Freshly ground black pepper
Lemon wedges, for squeezing over (optional)

Kakavia is the fishermen's soup. It's traditionally made with a medley of small fish and seafood caught in fishing nets that's not easily sold. This popular recipe is prepared all around the islands and is particularly beloved in the Dodecanese. On tiny islands, like Marathi, Arkioi and Pserimos, you can enjoy the best swims and savour the loveliest fish soups of your life. Beyond this version, fish soups are prepared in several other ways across the Greek islands, many of which are very light and summery. Some versions include rice, on Lesvos and Limnos they add *trahanas*, on Crete they grate fresh tomato in it, while others like to enrich it with *avgolemono* (egg and lemon sauce).

One of my favourite soups prepared on Paros includes both rice and *avgolemono*. It evokes memories of childhood summers with my grandfather. I remember going to the taverna on the seafront of Ambelas village with him to preorder the soup for the next day. The fish would be freshly caught, cooked within hours and served on a platter with the vegetables, while the broth with rice was poured directly into our plates.

Wash and dry the fish, then rub it all over with half a lemon and season with salt.

Pour 2 litres (68fl oz) of water into a large pan with a lid. Add the onion, leaf celery, tomato, peppercorns and allspice berries, if using, to the pan. Salt the water. Lower the fish into the water, making sure it is just covered; if necessary, add more water. Place the pot over a medium-high heat, cover with a lid and bring to the boil. Reduce the heat to low and gently simmer for 20 minutes, skimming off any foam that forms on the surface. Using a slotted spoon, carefully lift the fish out of the pan and transfer it to a serving platter. Cover to keep warm.

Add the carrots, potatoes and courgettes to the pot, then continue to simmer over a low heat for about 20 minutes or until the vegetables are cooked. Using a slotted spoon, remove the cooked vegetables from the pot and place them on a platter or in a bowl. Cover to keep warm.

Strain the cooking liquid through a fine sieve (strainer). Return this broth to the pot, then taste and adjust the seasoning, if needed. Bring the broth to the boil, add the rice and simmer over a low heat for a further 10–15 minutes or until the rice is al dente. Set aside 3 or 4 ladlefuls of hot broth for the sauce.

To make the sauce, beat the eggs in a bowl until very frothy, then vigorously whisk in the lemon juice. While whisking continuously, gradually pour in a little of the reserved hot broth. Once all the broth has been incorporated into the sauce, pour it into the pan with the soup and cook over a low heat, gently stirring, for a further 3–5 minutes. Taste and adjust the seasoning, if needed. Remove the pan from the heat and let the soup stand for 10 minutes while you prepare the fish.

Ladle the soup into deep bowls, equally dividing the fish and vegetables. Finish with freshly ground black pepper and a squeeze of lemon, if preferred.

Grilled sea bream wrapped in fig leaves

FROM **EVIA**

SERVES 2

- 4–6 fig leaves (depending on their size)
- 1 whole sea bream (or you can use sea bass, grouper, red snapper or trout), about 600g (1lb 5oz), scaled and cleaned
- ½ lemon
- 3–4 thyme sprigs
- 1 rosemary sprig
- Salt
- Olive oil

FOR THE SAUCE

- 50ml (1¾fl oz) fresh lemon juice
- 150ml (5fl oz) early harvest olive oil (or good-quality extra virgin olive oil)
- ½ teaspoon dried oregano
- Salt and freshly ground black pepper

TO SERVE

- Boiled or blanched foraged greens (or other greens)

Nestled in the Aegean Sea, Evia (also spelt Euboea) is a captivating island known for its majestic mountains and agricultural heritage. As the second-largest island after Crete, Evia is celebrated for its fertile land that produces exceptional cheeses and wines. The island is embraced by 800 kilometres of crystal blue waters, harbouring an abundance of fish and seafood. Among its treasures, the sea bream of Evia stands out, renowned for its exceptional quality and a favourite choice for grilled fish among Greeks.

Evia's figs are also legendary. These figs are so special that they hold a Protected Designation of Origin (PDO) certification, making them some of the finest in all of Greece. The fig leaves, although not edible themselves, have found their way into contemporary cooking. They are perfect for wrapping meats, fish and cheeses, adding a subtle flavour while keeping the food moist and tender during baking or grilling.

A classic accompaniment to grilled fish is horta (foraged greens). These greens are typically boiled or blanched and served as a refreshing salad, drizzled with high-quality olive oil and a splash of lemon juice. In the summer, I love using monk's beard or amaranth greens to perfectly complement fresh grilled fish.

First, wash the fig leaves and trim their stems. Blanch any larger or rougher leaves to make them softer and fold more easily. Bring a large pan of water to the boil and prepare a bowl of iced water. Gently submerge the leaves in the boiling water for 1 minute, then swiftly transfer them to the iced water to stop the cooking process. Leave to cool for 1 minute, then drain the leaves and pat dry with paper towels. Lay the leaves out on a clean surface, overlapping slightly to create a bed for the fish.

Clean the fish and pat dry with paper towels. Using a sharp knife, gently score the skin a few times on each side, taking care not to cut too deeply into the flesh. Rub the fish inside and out with half a lemon, then season with salt and stuff the cavity with the fresh herbs. Lay the sea bream on top of the prepared fig leaves and wrap them around the fish to seal it in a neat parcel – use additional leaves, if needed. Secure the parcel with kitchen twine.

Preheat your grill (broiler) to medium-high, around 200°C/400°F. If using a barbecue, make sure the coals are white hot and evenly spread. Cook the fish parcel for 10–12 minutes on each side under the grill or 8–10 minutes on each side on the barbecue. The fig leaves will char and infuse the fish with a subtle flavour. If grilling the fish unwrapped, reduce the grilling time by 2 minutes per side.

Meanwhile, prepare the sauce. Put the lemon juice in a bowl, then vigorously whisk in the olive oil. Season with the oregano, salt and pepper to taste. Set aside.

Once cooked, remove the fish from the grill or barbecue and leave to rest for a few minutes before unwrapping. The fig leaves are not to be eaten. Drizzle the fish with the sauce and serve with the foraged greens or your choice of side dish.

Bianco **Sea bass with potatoes, garlic and olive oil**

FROM **CORFU**

SERVES 4

1 whole sea bass, about 800g (1lb 12oz)
4 potatoes, about 900g (1lb 15oz)
80ml (2¾fl oz) olive oil
6–7 garlic cloves, peeled and sliced into thin slivers
2–3 fresh parsley sprigs
1 teaspoon dried oregano
50ml (1¾fl oz) dry white wine
3 tablespoons fresh lemon juice
2–3 tablespoons roughly chopped parsley
Salt and freshly ground black pepper

One of Corfu's most celebrated dishes is a simple yet delightful recipe featuring fish and potatoes braised in local olive oil. The island's abundant olive groves produce exceptional olive oils, with the native Lianolia variety being especially prized for its smooth, delicate flavour. In this dish, the fish is steamed rather than braised, resting on a bed of potatoes that cook slowly in the broth while the fish cooks. Ideal choices for this recipe include white fish such as sea bass, grouper, cod or pollock. The presence of bones and skin is crucial, as they release collagen that naturally thickens the sauce (and tightens the skin!), which is why traditional recipes often include the fish head as well. Similar recipes can be found throughout the Ionian Islands, including Lefkada, where the local variation features salted cod. If you'd like to try this version, be sure to thoroughly desalinate the salted cod before following this recipe.

Wash the whole sea bass and pat it dry with paper towels. Slicing through the spine, cut the fish into four steaks, each about 3cm (1 inch) thick. Set aside the head. Season the sea bass steaks with salt and black pepper.

Peel the potatoes and slice them into 1.5cm (½ inch) thick rounds. Heat the oil in a large, shallow pot or deep pan with a lid over a medium-high heat. Add the potatoes, then season with salt and pepper. Sauté the potatoes, turning them occasionally, until lightly golden. Add the garlic, parsley sprigs and dried oregano, then give the pan a gentle shake to mix everything.

Arrange the sea bass steaks on top of the potatoes, then pour in the wine and let it infuse. Next, add enough water to just cover the potatoes but not the fish. If you want, add the reserved fish head to the pan to add extra flavour to the stock. Cover the pan with a lid and gently simmer over a low heat for 15 minutes or until the fish is cooked through. Transfer the sea bass steaks to a platter and keep warm. Remove and discard the fish head, if using.

Check the potatoes. If they need more time, cook them uncovered for a further few minutes, but be careful not to overcook them as they may fall apart. Once the potatoes are ready, move them to the platter alongside the fish.

Reduce the sauce by continuing to simmer over a low heat. Remove and discard the parsley sprigs, then stir in the lemon juice and parsley. Cook for a further 5–10 minutes over a low heat until the sauce has nicely thickened.

Divide the potatoes between serving plates, then place a sea bass steak on top of each one. Spoon the sauce over the fish. Enjoy with good bread.

THE SPONGE DIVERS OF KALYMNOS

Part of the Dodecanese island group, Kalymnos is situated in the south-eastern Aegean Sea. It is a serene island, characterised by its dry, rocky terrain, idyllic beaches and crystal waters, with a reputation for exceptional climbing and fantastic local seafood.

The island's ruggedness and limited local resources have traditionally led its inhabitants to rely heavily on the sea and its abundant surrounding seabed. The local community has deep-rooted connections to the sea, with a heritage steeped in skilled fishing and sponge diving. These expert seafarers venture to great depths in search of sponges, often uncovering other precious seafood treasures along the way.

The island's cuisine is centred predominantly around fresh fish and seafood, including octopus fritters. However, Kalymnos is also famous for spinialo, a traditional preservation technique. Spinialo involves preserving seafood, typically local bivalves called fouskes (which are rather like oysters) that hide among the rocks and require adept divers to spot and harvest them.

Traditionally, this delicacy was prepared aboard fishing boats. After careful cleaning, the bivalves are cut and packed into sterilised bottles, immersed in brine made from seawater and extra salt, then finally topped with olive oil to prevent oxygen entering the bottle. The bottles are expertly sealed with corks and artistically wrapped with white and blue striped rope for added security and good luck. When properly managed, this method enhances the flavour of the bivalves and ensures their long-lasting preservation. Other seafood, such as sea urchins and limpets, are preserved using an identical method.

Spinialo is commonly served as an appetiser or meze, often garnished with roughly chopped or sliced onions, drizzled with olive oil and a squeeze of lemon juice, for those who so wish.

During the early twentieth century, a significant number of Kalymnians migrated to Tarpon Springs, Florida, USA, along with others from the Dodecanese islands. This migration started in 1905 when Greek immigrant John Cocoris introduced sponge diving to the Florida area. He recruited divers from Kalymnos and neighbouring Greek islands, which led to the establishment of a vibrant Greek community in Tarpon Springs. This migration played a crucial role in shaping Tarpon Springs into a prominent centre of Greek-American culture and a hub for the sponge-diving industry.

5€

Astakomakaronada **Lobster spaghetti with a quick tomato sauce**

FROM **SKYROS**

SERVES 2–4

1 live lobster (or use frozen lobster, thawed)
350g (12½oz) spaghetti or linguini

FOR THE SAUCE

3 tablespoons olive oil
2 garlic cloves, peeled and minced
2 bay leaves
1–2 small basil sprigs
130ml (4½fl oz) dry white wine
500g (1lb 2oz) tomatoes, grated (shredded) or skinned and chopped, fresh or store-bought
15g (½oz) butter
1–2 tablespoons chopped basil leaves
Sea salt and freshly ground black pepper

On the islands, pasta is frequently paired with lobster. This might sound extravagant, but it was traditionally a poor man's dish – a practical way to use available resources. Across the groups, several islands with a strong fishing tradition are famous for their lobsters and *astakomakaronada*, including Kythira, Milos, Koufonisi, Fournoi, as well as the area around Sporades with Skyros standing out. Lying a bit remote, Skyros is a fascinating island with a tranquillity I adore. Famous for its traditional crafts, wonderful carnival and excellent seafood, Skyros is a great destination for relaxing family holidays combining beautiful beaches and great food.

For this recipe, the lobster is cooked whole as the head holds much of the flavour. If you prefer, you can cook just the tails, following the same steps. The pasta traditionally used is spaghetti, but linguini also works great. You can use orzo, as is often done on Limnos. Depending on the season, prawns (shrimp), langoustines and slipper lobsters are used, so you may easily adapt the recipe to substitute any of these.

Before cooking the live lobster, place it in the freezer for 1 hour to slow its metabolism and 'put it to sleep'. Meanwhile, fill a large saucepan with 4 litres (4 quarts) of water and bring it to the boil. Season the water well with plenty of salt – this water will be used to cook the lobster, boil the pasta and be added to the sauce as well.

Take the lobster out of the freezer, lay it on a chopping board and insert a knife between the eyes to kill it, cutting right down through the head. Lower the lobster into the boiling water and cook for 8–10 minutes, depending on its size. The shell will turn red, while the meat inside should be white. Carefully remove the lobster from the pan and let it cool slightly. Using a slotted spoon, remove all the white parts of the lobster's flesh.

Using the same water, cook the pasta for 2 minutes less than stated on the packet instructions. Drain the pasta, reserving some of the cooking liquid for the sauce. Set aside.

Meanwhile, using special scissors or a large knife, cut the lobster in half lengthwise. You can remove the meat from the head to add to the sauce. Either leave the lobster tails in the shell or remove and cut the tails into smaller pieces to stir into the sauce, if you prefer. Cover and keep warm.

Recipe continues overleaf

To prepare the sauce, place a large, deep pan over a medium heat. Add the olive oil and sauté the garlic, bay leaves and basil, stirring for 2–3 minutes. Add the wine, giving it a few seconds for the alcohol to infuse, then add the tomatoes. Season with salt and black pepper.

Add the reserved lobster meat to the pan with the sauce. Reduce the heat to low, add 3–4 tablespoons of the cooking liquid and gently simmer, stirring occasionally, for about 4 minutes or until the sauce starts to thicken. Remove and discard the basil sprigs and bay leaves.

Add the cooked pasta to the pan and toss in the sauce. Allow everything to simmer together for 1 minute, adding a little more of the cooking liquid when needed, a tablespoon at a time, to keep the sauce juicy. Add the butter and stir until melted. Mix in the basil and freshly ground black pepper.

Arrange the pasta on a serving platter. Nestle the lobster tails, shell side down, in the remaining sauce in the pan to heat them up bit and release more flavour. Spoon the sauce over the pasta and place the lobster tails on top. Serve with some extra black pepper, if you like.

Psari spetsiota **Baked cod fillets with tomatoes, potatoes, courgettes and onions**

FROM **SPETSES**

SERVES 4

500g (1lb 2oz) potatoes, peeled and cut into 1cm (⅓ inch) slices
280g (10oz) courgettes (zucchini), trimmed and sliced lengthways into 1cm (⅓ inch) thick ribbons
Olive oil, for brushing
4 cod fillets, each weighing around 200–250g (7–9oz), fresh or frozen and defrosted

FOR THE SAUCE
2 onions, peeled, halved and thinly sliced
70ml (2½fl oz) olive oil
2 garlic cloves, peeled and thinly sliced
1 dried red chilli
1 bay leaf
150ml (5fl oz) dry white wine
580g (1lb 4oz) cherry tomatoes, blended until smooth
½ teaspoon dried oregano
Parsley
Salt and freshly ground black pepper

Nestled in the Saronic Gulf near the northeast of the Peloponnese, Spetses enchants visitors. The Venetians once called it Isola di Spezie, or Spice Island, thanks to the island's aromatic herbs and flowers and that's how its name became Spetses. With its rich history, striking architecture and cosmopolitan flair, Spetses offers a peaceful atmosphere where motor vehicles are rare. People get around on foot, by bicycle, by motorcycle or in horse-drawn carriages, which only adds to its old-world charm.

Arriving by ferry, your first glimpse of Spetses is Dapia, the historic square that serves as the main port, a picturesque harbour lined with cafes, tavernas and shops. The island's cuisine focuses on fish and seafood, with *spetsiota* being a local specialty. Fish is cooked in a simple tomato sauce, which can be baked whole, sliced into steaks or filleted. I like to add potatoes and courgettes (zucchini) to make it a full meal. For a more versatile version, skip the vegetables and simply bake the fish in the sauce – you can then serve the fish with other sides, such as rice or mashed potatoes.

Preheat the oven to 200°C/180°C fan/400°F/gas 6.

Brush a 23 x 30cm (9 x 12 inch) ovenproof dish with some of the olive oil, then lay the potato slices in a single layer over the base of the dish. Brush the potato slices with more olive oil, then sprinkle with salt and pepper. Bake on the middle rack of the hot oven for 10 minutes. Remove the dish from the oven, arrange the courgette ribbons on top of the potatoes in a second layer, then brush with more olive oil and season with salt and pepper. Return the dish to the oven and bake for a further 20–25 minutes or until the courgettes are tender.

Meanwhile, prepare the sauce. Heat a large pan over a medium-high heat and add 2 tablespoons of the olive oil. Sauté the onions with a pinch of salt until golden, then add the garlic, dried chilli and bay leaf and cook until softened.

Pour in the wine, let it simmer to cook off the alcohol, then add the puréed tomatoes. Stir, reduce the heat to medium-low, then season with salt and pepper. Simmer for 10–15 minutes until thickened, then add 40ml (3 tablespoons) of the olive oil and the dried oregano. Cook for a further 3–4 minutes. Remove the pan from the heat. Remove and discard the bay leaf and chilli, then stir in the parsley.

Once the potatoes are ready, remove the dish from the oven and spoon over half the sauce. Season the cod fillets with salt and pepper, then place them on top of the vegetables (skin side down, if applicable). Cover the fish with the remaining sauce. Drizzle over 1–2 tablespoons of olive oil and add some extra black pepper. Return the dish to the oven and bake for a further 15 minutes or until the fish is cooked through. Garnish the dish some with extra parsley, if you like.

Karavides me kolokythakia **Langoustines with courgettes**

FROM **SKIATHOS**

SERVES 2–4

- 8 whole langoustines or large prawns (jumbo shrimp) in their shells and ideally with head on (around 500g/1lb 2oz), fresh or frozen and defrosted
- 80ml (2¾fl oz) olive oil
- 1 large onion, peeled and roughly chopped
- 2–3 garlic cloves, peeled and roughly chopped
- 2 bay leaves
- 8 small courgettes (zucchini), trimmed but left whole
- 70ml (2½fl oz) white wine
- 550g (1lb 4oz) ripe tomatoes, grated (you should have about 450g/1lb grated tomato with juices)
- 4–5 tablespoons finely chopped parsley
- 3 tablespoons fresh lemon juice
- Salt and freshly ground black pepper

This dish hails from Skiathos, another island of the Northern Sporades located between Skopelos, Evia and mainland Greece, a region rich in fish and seafood. The cuisine here is heavily centred around the treasures of the sea, reflecting the area's variety of seafood and shellfish. Traditionally, fishermen would trade their catches with local farmers for olive oil and vegetables. As a result, the local cuisine evolved to prominently feature seafood, cooked alongside vegetables and foraged greens.

It's common to find local dishes that combine these ingredients in delightful ways, such as these langoustines with courgettes (zucchini) or lobster with foraged greens and herbs, such as chervil or fennel fronds. I adore this recipe, especially the way the courgettes are prepared. Even when you don't have langoustines or prawns (shrimp) to hand, you can still enjoy this dish using just courgettes.

Keep the langoustines whole and in their shells for more flavour and a messier, enjoyable eating experience. If you prefer not to have them whole, you can cook just the bodies, either in their shells or shelled. (If you remove the shells, cook them for 2 minutes less.)

Place a large, shallow pot or deep pan with a fitted lid over a medium heat. Add the olive oil and sauté the onion and garlic with the bay leaves for 2–3 minutes, stirring until soft. Add in the whole courgettes and season with salt and pepper. Sauté the courgettes for a couple of minutes on each side.

Pour in the wine, wait for the alcohol to evaporate, then add in the grated (shredded) tomatoes. Season with more salt and black pepper and gently simmer, with the lid slightly ajar, over a low heat for 15 minutes or until the courgettes are almost cooked (the cooking time will depend on the size of the courgettes).

Arrange the langoustines on top of the courgettes and cover again. Cook for a further 6–8 minutes or until their shells turn brighter in colour. Add in the lemon juice and chopped parsley and shake the pan to mix. Remove from heat and serve immediately.

Psito calamari **Grilled squid with herby rice**

FROM **HYDRA**

SERVES 4–6

FOR THE SKEWERS

1kg (2lb 4oz) whole squid, washed, cleaned and cut into 3cm (1 inch) rings
1 large yellow bell pepper, cut into 3cm (1 inch) pieces
12–15 baby plum tomatoes
12–15 caper leaves (optional)

FOR THE MARINADE

80ml (2¾fl oz) olive oil
100ml (3½fl oz) dry white wine
½ teaspoon salt
1 teaspoon freshly ground black pepper
1–2 thyme sprigs

FOR THE RICE

2 tablespoons olive oil
2–3 spring onions (scallions), chopped
750g (1lb 10oz) leftover basmati rice (or 250g/9oz uncooked rice)
2–3 tablespoons chopped dill
Salt and freshly ground black pepper

FOR THE DRESSING

70ml (2½fl oz) fresh lemon juice
1 teaspoon yellow mustard
150ml (5fl oz) olive oil
2–3 dill sprigs, chopped
Salt and freshly ground black pepper

A cosmopolitan gem, Hydra lies about 45 miles (70 kilometres) southwest of Athens. Motor vehicles are prohibited on the island, so transportation is primarily by foot, donkey or water taxi, contributing to its unspoiled atmosphere.

With daily catches, Hydra's squid is a local delicacy, enjoyed grilled, fried or stewed. For me, nothing compares to freshly grilled calamari dressed in olive oil and lemon, so here it is prepared and as souvlaki with yellow bell peppers, baby tomatoes and caper leaves. I serve these skewers with a rice dish that pairs well with seafood and is a perfect way to use up leftover rice. The inspiration for this recipe is a rice dish that I have been eating for years at Tarsanas restaurant on Tinos – I love it.

The *ladolemono* dressing may be used for all sorts of seafood and salads. You can store it in the fridge, just let it come to room temperature and shake the jar well before use.

First, make the marinade. Combine the olive oil, wine, salt and pepper in a large bowl, then add the thyme. Toss the calamari rings in the marinade, coating them well, then cover the bowl and chill in the fridge for 1 hour.

Soak six bamboo skewers in cold water for 30 minutes to prevent burning, or use metal skewers. Thread the calamari onto the prepared skewers, alternating with pieces of yellow bell pepper, baby tomatoes and caper leaves, if using.

For the dressing, combine the lemon juice and mustard in a bowl. Whisking vigorously, add the olive oil, season with salt and pepper, then stir in the dill.

Prepare the rice just before grilling the calamari. Place a non-stick pan over a medium heat. Once hot, add the olive oil and spring onions, stirring for 1 minute until slightly softened. Add the rice and dill, then season with salt and pepper. Lower the heat and cook, stirring, for 2–3 minutes until the rice looks fluffy and is piping hot all the way through. Remove from the heat, cover with a clean dish towel and place the lid on top to keep the rice warm and fluffy.

Meanwhile, preheat the barbecue or a grill pan over a medium-high heat. Once hot, place the skewers on the grill and cook for 3–4 minutes on each side, or until the calamari is opaque, slightly charred and has grill marks. Avoid overcooking as the calamari will turn chewy.

Spoon the rice onto serving plates, arrange the calamari skewers on top and drizzle over the dressing.

Meat

CHAPTER 4

Hoirino me pligouri **Pork with cumin, bulgur and chickpeas**

FROM **KOS**

SERVES 4

FOR THE PORK
600g (1lb 5oz) pork neck, cut into 3cm (1 inch) chunks
50ml (1¾fl oz) olive oil
1 tablespoon ground cumin
2 thyme sprigs
50ml (1¾fl oz) white wine
About 350–400ml (12–14fl oz) hot vegetable stock or water
3 tablespoons fresh lemon juice
Salt and freshly ground black pepper

FOR THE BULGUR
200g (7oz) bulgur (cracked) wheat
240ml (8½fl oz) boiling water
1 tablespoon butter
Salt

FOR THE CHICKPEAS
150g (5½oz) cooked chickpeas (garbanzo beans) or 80g/3oz dried chickpeas
1 small onion, chopped
1 teaspoon roughly chopped thyme leaves
¼ teaspoon ground cumin
¼ teaspoon salt
60ml (2fl oz) olive oil
Freshly ground black pepper, to taste

TO SERVE
Roughly chopped thyme leaves (optional)

Kos is an island renowned for its vast, fertile plains – a rare feature among Greek islands – making it an ideal hub for agriculture. It's especially notable for its tomatoes. From the 1960s to the 1980s, the local tomato industry flourished and both fresh and processed tomatoes were exported. Many islanders were employed in numerous processing units, providing a livelihood for much of the population. Since tourism took over as the island's main revenue, tomatoes were sadly put to one side. Apart from tomatoes, Kos is celebrated for its grapes, melons, cheeses and other dairy products. The island's agricultural landscape is also characterised by its emphasis on livestock farming, making the local cuisine centred more on meat than on seafood.

Pork holds a special place in the local cuisine of Kos, featuring prominently in traditional dishes. The island maintains the cultural practice of *choirosfagia*, an ancient custom of pig butchery carried out as a festival in the village of Pyli (see page 42). One straightforward dish from Kos involves pork generously seasoned with cumin, a popular spice throughout the Dodecanese region. This dish is typically served with bulgur (cracked) wheat, a staple grain on the island. Although bulgur is traditionally prepared without chickpeas (garbanzo beans), which are frequently used in recipes, I add them here as they complement the meat-centric meals enjoyed on the island.

If using dried chickpeas, soak them overnight. The next day, boil the chickpeas until soft – this typically takes 40–45 minutes, but the cooking time will vary depending on the quality and freshness of the chickpeas. (Adding a pinch of bicarbonate of soda or baking soda to the soaking water helps to soften the chickpeas as well.) Drain and leave to dry.

Season the pork with plenty of salt, then let stand at room temperature for 30 minutes before cooking. Heat a deep frying pan (skillet) with a well-fitting lid over medium-high heat and add the olive oil. Once hot, add the pork and cook, stirring, until brown on all sides. While stirring, add the ground cumin, thyme sprigs and plenty of black pepper. Pour in the wine and let the alcohol infuse the pork, then add enough hot stock or water to just cover the meat. Adjust the seasoning with more salt, if needed. Cover the pan with the lid, and when the liquid starts to simmer, reduce the heat to low and gently cook for 30 minutes.

Remove and discard the thyme sprigs. Stir in the lemon juice, then adjust the seasoning with salt and pepper to taste. Cover the pan again and continue to gently simmer for a further 10–15 minutes or until the pork is very tender and the sauce has slightly thickened.

Using a ladle, scoop out about 75ml (2½fl oz) of the cooking liquid from the pan and set aside. Remove the pan from the heat and keep covered and warm.

Meanwhile, prepare the bulgur wheat and chickpeas. Place the bulgur wheat in a large metal bowl and cover it with the boiling water. Add a pinch of salt, stir to mix well, then cover the bowl with a clean dish towel and let it soak for 10–15 minutes or until soft. Fluff the bulgur wheat with a fork, drain off any excess liquid and let it stand in a colander for 5–10 minutes to dry.

In a separate bowl, mix the chickpeas with the onions, thyme leaves, ground cumin, salt and plenty of black pepper to taste. Heat a pan over a medium-high heat and add the olive oil. Once hot, add the chickpea and onion mixture to the pan. Toss everything in the pan for a few minutes until the chickpeas are golden and slightly crispy. Transfer the chickpea and onion mixture to a bowl.

Using the same pan, add the tablespoon of butter and, once melted, mix in the bulgur wheat. Ladle the reserved pork cooking liquid into the bulgur wheat and cook, stirring, until the liquid is fully absorbed. Stir in the chickpea and onion mixture, adjust the seasoning to taste and remove the pan from heat.

When ready to serve, arrange the bulgur wheat and chickpea mixture over a serving platter, then spoon the stewed pork on top. Drizzle over the remaining sauce and, if using, scatter over the fresh thyme.

Kreatosoupa **Comforting beef soup with veggies**

FROM **ZAKYNTHOS**

SERVES 4–6

800g (1lb 12oz) braising steak (beef chuck)
300g (10½oz) bone from the beef, ideally with marrow (I ask my butcher to cut one)
1kg (2lb 4oz) very ripe tomatoes, cored
1 teaspoon fleur de sel
2 onions, peeled and quartered
3 celery stalks, cut into 2cm (⅔ inch) slices
2 carrots, cut into 2cm (⅔ inch) slices
4 potatoes, peeled and halved
Freshly ground black pepper

This recipe belongs to Eugenia Markesini Hobson, the executive chef and co-owner of Our Mom Eugenia, a Greek restaurant in Northern Virginia. Born and raised on the island of Zakynthos, Eugenia faced early hardships, being raised by her grandparents after losing her father and her mother emigrated to Germany for work. She spent her childhood learning to cook alongside her grandmother, after whom she was named. After school, Eugenia met John, her husband for over 50 years. After many years of working in other Greek restaurants around Washington D.C., she opened her first restaurant in 2016 with her sons Alexander and Philip. They have since expanded to three locations and have received glowing reviews from established publications such as the *Washington Post* and *Wall Street Journal*.

The cuisine of Zakynthos is renowned for its flavourful soups, prepared for casual meals and festive occasions. These range from quick summer tomato soups to fish, turkey, chicken and meat soups. They can be plain or enriched with *avgolemono* (egg and lemon sauce, see page 91), pasta or rice. Eugenia keeps this meat soup simple. It's her favourite dish, which has become the entire family's favourite too. Eugenia fondly recalls eating this soup as a child during summers in her village, made with the ripe, juicy tomatoes from her grandparents' garden. This soup is traditionally served with good crusty bread and *ladotyri* cheese from Zakynthos.

Cut the beef into individual portions, each weighing about 100g (3½oz). Ask your butcher to do this and reserve the bone (which is used later).

In a large bowl, squeeze the tomatoes hard with your hands. Knead them with 1 teaspoon of the fleur de sel. Reserve all the tomato juices. Set aside.

Place the beef and the bone in a large saucepan with a well-fitting lid. Pour in enough water to cover the meat, then place over a medium heat and bring to the boil. Using a slotted spoon, remove any foam that forms on the surface.

Add the crushed tomatoes to the pan, along with all their juices. Lower the heat, cover the pan with the lid, leaving it slightly ajar, and gently simmer for 45–50 minutes. Add the onions, celery, carrots and potatoes to the pan. If necessary, top up with enough warm water to cover all the vegetables. Adjust the seasoning with salt and black pepper, to taste. Continue to simmer for a further 35 minutes or until the vegetables have softened and the broth has reduced and thickened.

When ready to serve, ladle the soup into deep bowls, dividing the meat and vegetables equally between the bowls. Season with a little extra black pepper.

Arni sto fourno me patates **Classic roast lamb with potatoes, herbs and garlic**

FROM **LESVOS**

SERVES 4–6

1.7–2kg (4lb 8oz) lamb (or goat) on the bone and with skin on, washed and dried
130ml (4½fl oz) olive oil
2½ teaspoons dried oregano
4–5 potatoes
5 garlic cloves, peeled and sliced into thin slivers
4–5 small rosemary sprigs
Sea salt (finely ground)
Freshly ground black pepper
150ml (5fl oz) dry white wine
80ml (2½fl oz) fresh lemon juice
100ml (3½fl oz) water

Popular at Easter and during other festivities, this simple lamb roast is loved all over Greece. On many islands, such as Folegandros, Ikaria and Nisyros, this dish is offered at *panigyria* (outdoor festivals, see page 86) and traditional weddings. Lesvos is an island known for the high quality of sheep bred there, making it one of the islands where lamb is abundant for popular recipes. At home, roasts like this are very simply cooked, usually with plenty of garlic, lemon and wine or a grape distillate such as *tsikoudia* from Crete. As the dish contains very few ingredients, fresh herbs and sea salt make the difference

For this recipe, try to source good-quality lamb. It can be any part of the lamb: I particularly like the shoulder and ribs, but the leg is also great. Greek lambs are small and quite lean. This is why when Greeks roast lamb, they keep the meat in one piece and they ask the butcher to 'break it', meaning to score it and break some bones so it can easily fit in the baking pan and is easier to serve when cooked. You can also cut it into portions, but make sure they are not too small to avoid drying out.

Trim away any excess fat on the lamb and massage it with 1 tablespoon of the olive oil, 1½ teaspoons of the dried oregano and salt and pepper. Drizzle a deep roasting tray (sheet pan) with 2 tablespoons of the olive oil. Place the lamb in the tray and let it stand at room temperature for 20–30 minutes before cooking.

Meanwhile, peel the potatoes, cut them in half lengthwise and then cut each half again lengthwise. Add to a large bowl and mix with 1 tablespoon of olive oil, the remaining oregano, about 1 teaspoon of salt and black pepper. Arrange the potatoes around the lamb.

Put the garlic slivers in a small bowl and mix with a pinch of salt and black pepper. Using a sharp knife, create 10–12 small slits randomly over the meat and insert a seasoned garlic sliver into each slit. Squeeze the remaining garlic slivers between the potatoes and meat, then scatter the rosemary sprigs over the top.

Preheat the oven to 200°C/180°C fan/400°F/gas 6.

In a small jug (pitcher), mix the wine, lemon juice and remaining olive oil with 100ml (3½fl oz) water, then pour over the meat and potatoes. Cover with a lid or parchment paper, sealed on top with foil. Roast on a low rack for 30 minutes, then reduce the heat to 170°C/150°C fan/325°F/gas 3 and roast for a further 1½ hours. Uncover the meat and spoon the sauce from the pan over the meat and potatoes, avoiding stirring. Continue to roast for another 40 minutes depending on the size of the meat and the cut, or until the lamb is well browned and potatoes are golden. Remove from the oven, let stand for 10–15 minutes loosely covered with parchment paper, then slice and serve.

Kotopoulo tserepa **Slow-roast chicken with potatoes**

FROM **ITHACA**

SERVES 4

- 4 chicken thighs with drumsticks attached (about 1.5kg/3lb 5oz), rinsed and dried
- 140ml (4½fl oz) olive oil
- 1 large onion, peeled
- 2 Romano peppers (or red bell peppers)
- 2 tomatoes (about 400g/14oz), peeled and cored
- 70ml (6fl oz) white wine
- 3 tablespoons fresh lemon juice
- 3–4 garlic cloves, peeled and roughly chopped or thinly sliced
- 3 potatoes (around 650g/1lb 6oz), peeled and quartered lengthwise
- 3–4 fresh marjoram sprigs or 1½ teaspoons dried marjoram
- Salt and freshly ground black pepper

This dish is named after a unique cooking implement, a dome-shaped, heavy lid called a *tserepa*. Used on an open fire, the *tserepa* was fitted over a baking pan to act as a multi-purpose, mobile oven. The pan would be heated over hot coals, then the *tserepa* fitted on top and a few coals placed on the lid to ensure even cooking. Traditional *tserepas* were typically made of clay mixed with goat hair to strengthen the dome and prevent cracking. Nomadic shepherds, farm workers, labourers and others without access to a regular oven would take the *tserepa* with them to prepare bread, pies or roast meats, and particularly chicken. It was an essential utensil in the countryside on Ithaca, Kefalonia and Lefkada, as well as parts of mainland Greece.

You can use a whole chicken or specific cuts like thighs or drumsticks, all with skin and bones intact. I find thighs with drumsticks attached to be ideal. The longer you cook this dish, the better the flavour develops. I've cooked it for up to 6 hours, which resulted in the best version so far. I offer two cooking methods: a slow version also suitable for wood-burning ovens and open fires, plus a faster version for convenience.

Preheat the oven to either 170°C/150°C fan/325°F/gas 3 to slow cook or 190°C/170°C fan/375°F/gas 5 for a faster cooking time.

Rub the chicken thighs with a little olive oil and season generously with salt and black pepper. Arrange in a large, deep ovenproof dish.

Cut the onion, peppers and tomatoes into rough 3cm (1 inch) chunks, place in a bowl and season with salt and black pepper. Scatter the vegetables around and between the chicken thighs, including the tomato juices from the bowl.

In a separate bowl, combine the olive oil, white wine and lemon juice. Whisk in the minced garlic, then season with salt and black pepper. Pour this mixture over the chicken and vegetables, then add the marjoram.

To ensure the dish cooks evenly and stays moist, first cover the ovenproof dish with parchment paper and then tightly seal it with a layer of foil. This traps in the steam during cooking and keeps the flavours locked in.

Place the dish in the hot oven and either slow cook it at 170°C/150°C fan/325°F/gas 3 for 5–6 hours or cook at 190°C/170°C fan/375°F/gas 5 for 2 hours or until the chicken and potatoes turn lightly golden and any liquid has significantly reduced. (If you need to speed up the roasting process even more, you can uncover the chicken after 1 hour and roast it for a further 45 minutes or until golden.) Once done, carefully remove the foil and parchment paper – taking care not to burn yourself on the steam – and rest for 15 minutes before serving.

Pastitsada **Beef stewed in a spicy tomato sauce served over pasta**

FROM **CORFU**

SERVES 4–6

1kg (2lb 4oz) beef for stewing, cut into small portions about 70–100g (2½–3½oz) each
60ml (2fl oz) olive oil
2 large onions, peeled and finely chopped
3 garlic cloves, peeled and minced
3 bay leaves
1 teaspoon *spetseriko* spice mix (see page 82)
1 teaspoon tomato paste (concentrated purée)
20ml (4 teaspoons) red wine vinegar
120ml (4½fl oz) sweet red wine, such as Mavrodaphne
1 thin sliver orange zest
1 small basil sprig, plus extra chopped to serve (optional)
250ml (9fl oz) tomato pulp or passata (strained tomatoes)
250ml (9fl oz) hot vegetable or meat stock or water
Salt and freshly ground black pepper

FOR THE PASTA
500g (1lb 2oz) bucatini (or any other pasta)
1–2 tablespoons olive oil
Grated *Kefalotiri*, pecorino or Parmesan

Every Greek island boasts its own version of stewed meat in tomato sauce, often served with a type of local pasta or fried potatoes. Known as *pastitsada*, on Corfu this dish takes on a special character thanks to the *spetseriko* (local spice mix). The name derives from the Italian word *spezie*, meaning spices. Traditionally, this blend was ground using a pestle and mortar and was prepared by pharmacists' assistants, locally known as *spetsierides*, particularly in the historic Karmela Deleonardou Pharmacy in the main town of Corfu, where locals would mainly source it for their Easter, Christmas and Sunday cooking. During summer they would also add it to spice up their local *sykomaida* (dried fig salami). Some believe the blend includes up to 12 spices, but often less are used and the ratios of the different spices in the blend vary. Paprika is important here, both sweet and spicy. Fennel seeds, cinnamon, cumin, clove, nutmeg, bay leaves, allspice and black pepper are also used. Some blends include ginger too.

Pastitsada is traditionally made with cockerel, but nowadays beef is used more often. The meat is served over bucatini-like pasta, but almost any kind of pasta works. Otherwise, rice or fried potatoes are delicious here too. Notable in this recipe is the vinegar, which is used aside from the wine. Vinegar plays a significant role in the Venetian essence of Corfiot cuisine, adding its distinctive touch to many dishes. I like to add a bit of orange zest and basil in the stew and I use sweet wine to avoid sugar. If you can't get sweet red wine, you may use a dry one and add a bit of sugar to taste. And the basil may be replaced with parsley, if that's more convenient.

First, make the *spetseriko*. Warm a clean, dry pan over a medium heat. Add the bay leaves, chilli flakes, fennel seeds and cumin to the pan and toss for 1–1½ minutes until lightly toasted and fragrant. Tip the toasted spices into a mortar and pestle or spice grinder and crush them to a fine powder. Mix in the ground spices and store in a sealed jar for up to 6 months.

Season the beef with salt and pepper and let it sit at room temperature for 30 minutes before cooking.

Place a large shallow pot over a medium-high heat. Add 3 tablespoons of the olive oil and, once hot, brown the meat on all sides. Using a slotted spoon, transfer the meat to a platter.

Recipe continues overleaf

FOR THE SPETSERIKO SPICE MIX

10 bay leaves
½ tablespoon chilli flakes
1 teaspoon fennel seeds
½ teaspoon cumin seeds
2 tablespoons sweet paprika
½ tablespoon spicy paprika
½ tablespoon ground cinnamon
½ teaspoon ground nutmeg
½ teaspoon ground cloves
½ teaspoon freshly ground black pepper
½ teaspoon ground allspice

In the same pot, add another tablespoon of olive oil and sauté the onions with a bit of salt until they turn light golden. Add in the garlic, bay leaves, and the *spetseriko* spice mix, stirring briefly. A few seconds later, add the tomato paste and stir gently. Return the browned meat to the pot, pour in the vinegar, and after a minute, pour in the wine. Allow the alcohol to evaporate for a couple of minutes, then pour in the tomato pulp and hot broth, and add in the orange zest and basil sprig. Reduce the heat to low, cover with a lid, and gently simmer for 50–60 minutes or until the meat is very tender and the sauce has thickened. Remove and discard the bay leaves, basil sprig and orange zest.

Cook the pasta according to the packet instructions. Drain and return the pasta to the pan, then add in a splash of olive oil and toss to coat.

Serve the beef with the sauce on top of the pasta, then sprinkle with some grated cheese and extra ground black pepper. If you like, scatter over a handful of chopped basil.

Samiotiko giouvetsi **Oven-baked orzo with ground beef**

FROM **SAMOS**

SERVES 6

FOR THE MEAT SAUCE
2 tablespoons olive oil
500g (1lb 2oz) minced (ground) beef (I use blade/shoulder)
1 onion, grated (shredded) or finely chopped
1 bay leaf
1 large carrot, grated (shredded)
2 garlic cloves, peeled and minced
¼ teaspoon ground cinnamon
1 teaspoon dried marjoram
120ml (4½fl oz) dry rose or white wine
200g (7oz) chopped tomatoes (fresh or canned)
2 tablespoons roughly chopped parsley

FOR THE ORZO
350g (12½oz) orzo
2 teaspoons butter
Olive oil, for greasing the dish
300g (10½oz) ripe tomatoes, skinned, deseeded and chopped
100g (3½oz) grated (shredded) *kefalotyri* or pecorino
Salt and freshly ground black pepper

Samos is a large island located in the eastern Aegean, very close to Turkey. It is a lush, mountainous island with fertile valleys, olive groves, vineyards, and pine forests. It is also home to waterfalls and habitats where wild birds such as herons and pink flamingos roost. Many refer to Samos as 'The Lady of the Vineyards' due to its long history of winemaking. The wines of Samos have been famous since antiquity; its unique climate and terrain contribute to the exceptional quality of its wines, particularly the Muscat grape, which thrives in the mountainous vineyards.

The cuisine of Samos shows a significant influence from Asia Minor due to the large number of Greeks who moved there from Smyrna (Izmir) and nearby areas in the early 1920s. Prepared throughout Greece, *giouvetsi* takes its name from the Turkish *güveç*, a clay pot used in Ottoman cuisine for casseroles and stews. In Greece, *giouvetsi* features orzo baked with meat, poultry or seafood stewed in a rich tomato sauce. On Samos, a unique variation involves a flavourful Bolognese-style sauce layered over the orzo. It's a comforting, delicious dish that's particularly popular with children.

First, make the meat sauce. Place a large, deep frying pan (skillet) over a medium-high heat. Heat the olive oil and gently brown the meat, stirring it with a spatula until browned. Add in the onion, bay leaf and carrot, season with some salt and pepper, and stir until the onion and carrot start to soften and the juices are mostly absorbed. Add in the garlic, gently mix for a minute, pour in the wine and give it a minute for the alcohol to evaporate. Then, add in the tomatoes, followed by the cinnamon and marjoram. (If the tomatoes you are using are not very flavourful, sprinkle them with a bit of sugar after you chop them.) Bring the heat down to low, cover and gently cook for 15–20 minutes until most of the liquid has been absorbed. Adjust seasoning, discard the bay leaf, and mix in the parsley.

While the sauce is cooking, boil the orzo in salted water for 2 minutes less than stated on the packet. Drain the orzo and return to the pot. Mix with the butter, salt (balance it with the cheese) and freshly ground black pepper to taste and 2–3 tablespoons of the cheese.

Preheat the oven to 200°C/180°C fan/400°F/gas 6.

Lightly grease a 27 x 20cm (9 x 7 inch) ovenproof dish with olive oil. Spread the orzo over the base of the prepared dish, spreading it out evenly. Ladle the meat sauce on top of the pasta, evening it out with the back of the ladle or a spatula. Finally, top it with the tomatoes and remaining cheese. Bake in the hot oven for 30 minutes or until golden. Let it cool down slightly before serving.

Kapriko me lemonofila **Slow-roast pork shoulder with lemon and fennel seeds**

FROM **CRETE**

SERVES 6–8

- 2kg (4lb 8oz) boneless pork shoulder (with skin on)
- 2 lemons, quartered
- 2–3 teaspoons sea salt
- 1 tablespoon fennel seeds
- 1 teaspoon freshly ground black pepper
- 4 garlic cloves, peeled and minced
- 2 tablespoons olive oil
- 8–10 fresh or frozen lemon leaves, slightly torn (or use lime leaves, but both are optional)
- Pinch of dried oregano

Lemon trees are prized not only for their fruit! Lemon leaves and blossoms also work beautifully in traditional recipes found around the Greek islands. On Tinos, for instance, they place warm *pastelia* (sesame honey bars) on top of lemon leaves to absorb their fragrance while they cool down and set. On other islands like Crete, bread is laid to cool or rusks to dry on a bed of lemon leaves, infusing them with their aroma. The blossoms are used in salads, a common practice in Crete during spring, and on Chios, they preserve the blossoms as a spoon sweet in syrup.

One of my favourite ways to use lemon leaves is in a roast. On Crete, this is a classic way to roast pork. *Kapriko* in particular refers to a male pig and is often served at festivals such as the *panigyri* of Saint Marina in mid-July in Heraklion. The leaves add a subtle citrus aroma to the meat, but I also add lemons and rub the pork with crushed fennel seeds. If you don't have access to a lemon tree, try using lime leaves. If you don't have access to any leaves, simply use an extra lemon. You can also add whole new potatoes, skin-on, to the pan and roast them with the pork – they are absolutely delicious! I like serving the roast meat and its divine crispy crackling with a simple, refreshing, lemony green salad that is rich in herbs. This is ideal for a Sunday or festive occasion as, although the recipe is very easy to prep, it does take some time.

Thoroughly dry the pork by patting it with paper towels. Score the pork skin in a criss-cross pattern or with parallel lines, taking care not to cut all the way through to the meat. (This will help the fat render and the skin become crispy.) Squeeze the juice of one lemon over the pork, ensuring it gets into the scored areas. Rub the pork with 2–3 tablespoons of sea salt, working it into the cuts. Let the pork stand at room temperature for 40–50 minutes.

Preheat the oven to 160°C/140°C/300°F/gas 2.

If the skin of the pork has become too wet, pat it dry again.

Finely grind the fennel seeds using a mortar and pestle or a food processor. Mix the ground fennel seeds, black pepper and minced garlic with just enough lemon juice to create a paste. Rub this paste onto the pork meat (avoiding the skin) and then squeeze some of the paste into the scored cuts of the skin, massaging it in.

Lay the fresh lemon leaves (or lime leaves), if using, on the bottom of a roasting tray (sheet pan) to form a bed for the pork. Mix the juice from two lemon quarters with the olive oil and any remaining fennel mixture and pour over the leaves in the pan. Place the pork on top of the leaves and arrange the squeezed lemon quarters and the remaining whole lemon quarters around the pork shoulder in the roasting tray.

Pour 150ml (5fl oz) water into the tray and place it on a low rack in the oven. Roast in the hot oven for 50 minutes, or until the skin starts to turn golden. Cover the pork loosely with parchment paper and continue to slow cook for a further 1–1½ hours, checking occasionally and basting the meat (not the skin) with the pan juices.

Remove the pork from the oven and let it rest for 10 minutes. (This rest period helps redistribute the juices within the meat.)

Increase the oven temperature to 220°C/200°C fan/425°F/gas 7.

Return the pork to the oven and roast for a further 15–20 minutes or until the skin is bubbly, crispy and golden brown. Once cooked, remove the pork from the oven and sprinkle it with a pinch of dried oregano. Let it rest for 15–20 minutes before slicing. Crack the cracklings into smaller pieces and carve the meat. Serve the meat drizzled with its sauce, along with the cracklings and a side salad, potatoes or steamed vegetables.

PANIGYRIA – *The Island Festivals*

To truly grasp the essence of Greek island living and the remarkable vitality of its inhabitants, you must dive deep into the panigyria. These age-old celebrations are the soulful gatherings that breathe life into villages, pulsating with the rhythm of communal joy. They are usually held outdoors, in a central square or around a church. Often, they take place in unexpected or remote locations – even on uninhabited islands, where there is a chapel – providing a reason to gather and celebrate.

A panigyri usually celebrates a saint, and there are enough saints to celebrate each and every day! Some festivals are dedicated to local produce or the making of a food or drink that the island is well known for. June sees an artichoke festival on Tinos. A sardine festival is held in July or early August on Lesvos, where hundreds of sardines are grilled outdoors. In August, they celebrate their local lentil in Lefkada. On Chios, they organise a fiesta for their precious mastiha. And on Samos and Lemnos, they celebrate local wines. Although these festivals have been Christianised over time, their roots are pagan, with Dionysian elements traced back to ancient Greece.

The word panigyri is derived from the ancient Greek panigyris, meaning ‘a general gathering’. Greeks haven’t stopped using the term ever since. This term is literal as the festivals are open to everyone, from infants to elders, regardless of the hour or how crowded it may be. In simple terms, panigyria provide the opportunity for people of all ages and backgrounds to gather, feast, drink, dance and let loose. I call it group therapy because I think you see the world differently after experiencing one of these events.

Food is central to a panigyri, with the entire village participating in preparing the feast. The dishes served showcase key aspects of the local cuisine. For larger festivals, the food is often cooked on site in massive pots lined up outdoors. Feasts frequently feature meats, usually goat, mutton, lamb or pork, depending on the island. This tradition can be traced to ancient rituals of sacrificing an animal in honour of a god, a practice that evolved to include the Saints of the Christian church, although the sacrifice is mostly symbolic nowadays.

The meat is prepared in various ways: sometimes a whole goat or lamb is stuffed and baked overnight in a wood-burning oven, or the meat might be stewed and served with pasta or potatoes. Alternatively, it could be made into a soup or stock, then used to enhance the flavours in dishes with rice, wheat or pulses. A culinary masterpiece of Crete is antikristo, a traditional method for roast goat or lamb; the meat is butterflied or cut into large pieces, seasoned with salt, and skewered on large wooden rods arranged in a circular fashion around an open fire. Slow-roasted for several hours, the result is simply heavenly!

Some islands offer seafood. On Koufonisi they fry fresh fish to offer to everyone. On Amorgos they fry cod or smelt. And on Santorini, at the festival of Saint Matrona in October, salt cod is served with onions and boiled potatoes.

Pies, sausages, cheeses and other delicacies, as well as pitchers of local wine, feature prominently on long tables arranged around the central dancing area. At most panigyria, the menu remains consistent year after year, becoming an anticipated tradition: for instance, the clay pot-baked chickpeas (garbanzo beans) served on Sifnos and Nisyros or the legendary dourmaes – slim rolls of grape leaves filled with minced meat and rice – served at festivals on Kasos. I can eat a dozen dourmaes in mere minutes. Food is essential as it lines the stomach before the large amounts of alcohol that are often consumed at these events. Then, after the food, comes the dancing!

Music is crucial as it sets the mood. Everyone eagerly joins the dance, which lasts until the sun has risen. The music is live, featuring mostly traditional island songs. Just as food, architecture and local crafts vary from island to island, so does music. Popular at festivals are songs and dances from the island of Ikaria, featuring a fast-paced, circular style of dancing that is described as bringing dancers into a trance-like state. The most famous panigyri on Ikaria is held on 6th August in the mountainous village of Raches.

When the festival is associated with a saint, a mass is held and the saint's image is then paraded through the village in a procession ending where the panigyri takes place. The most legendary panigyria are held in August, mainly on the 15th, in honour of the Virgin Mary. Each year, over 20,000 festivals take place that day. Some of the most legendary annual panigyria are on Paros, Ikaria, Lesvos, Alonnisos, Andros, Tinos, Thasos, Kalimnos, Fournoi and Chios, to name only some islands. Some of these celebrations take it even further, lasting several days. For example, festivals on Serifos and Astypalea span three days, while the one on Nisyros extends to a remarkable nine days!

On Karpathos and Crete, where local traditions are preserved, the panigyri showcases cultural heritage. The focus is on distinctive local music, played on folk instruments such as the lyra, laouto, and tsambouna, accompanied by unique dances. It's common to see locals dressed in traditional attire, including the iconic sariki, the black headgear worn on Crete, or the flower-patterned scarves and golden jewellery from Karpathos.

At the heart of these festivals, I've found myself immersed in moments of pure joy. Beyond the delicious food, endless pours and lively dances, what really stands out is the collective energy that electrifies the atmosphere. Among the bustling crowds, I've made new friends and shared laughs and stories like we've known each other forever. These gatherings are full of energy and warmth, where the simple act of hugging someone feels like reuniting with family. Underneath the stars, surrounded by cheerful faces, you can sense the deep bond that connects us all, making these celebrations truly special.

Patatato **Goat and potato stew with wine and thyme**

FROM **AMORGOS**

SERVES 4

1kg (2lb 4oz) goat shoulder or leg, with bone, cut into 4 portions
5 tablespoons olive oil
300g (10½oz) chopped onions
2 garlic cloves, peeled and roughly chopped
1 tomato, peeled, deseeded and diced
7 allspice berries
2 bay leaves
10 fresh thyme sprigs, tied with kitchen twine
1 cinnamon stick
1 tablespoon tomato paste (concentrated purée)
150ml (5fl oz) dry rosé or white wine
900ml (30fl oz) hot stock
Salt and freshly ground black pepper

FOR THE POTATOES
1kg (2lb 4oz) potatoes (of similar size and shape)
Olive oil, for frying
Salt and freshly ground black pepper

On 26th July each year, Amorgos hosts the largest *panigyri* (outdoor festival, see page 86) of the Cycladic islands, dedicated to the island's patron saint, Agia Paraskevi. Food is a key aspect of the celebration, with locals contributing substantial quantities of meat, wheat and potatoes to fulfil the feasting requirements. Preparation begins days beforehand, involving extensive cooking, including breadmaking.

Among the dishes served, the star attraction is *patatato* (meaning 'potatoey'), a slow-cooked meat stew with potatoes and wine. It's typically made with goat meat, but lamb or beef can also be used. As many as 20 massive pots of the stew are offered, immediately following the church service. When I stew goat or lamb, I prefer to use shoulder. Meat cooked on the bone tends to be tender, moist and tastier, thanks to the collagen that breaks down during cooking, resulting in a better texture.

Wash the goat meat, pat dry with paper towels and season with salt and pepper. Heat 4 tablespoons of the olive oil in a wide, shallow pan over a medium–high heat. Add the meat and brown well on all sides. Transfer to a plate and set aside.

Over a medium heat, add the remaining tablespoon of olive oil to the pan. Add the onion with a pinch of salt and sauté until soft. Add the garlic, tomato, allspice berries, bay leaves, thyme sprigs and cinnamon stick and sauté for 1 minute until the tomato is soft. Squeeze in the tomato paste, stirring to combine, and return the goat to the pan, turning it until covered with the sauce. Pour in the wine, allow the alcohol to evaporate, then pour in 900ml (30fl oz) of the hot stock to just cover the meat and season with salt and pepper. Cover with a lid left slightly ajar. Once simmering, reduce the heat to low and cook for 40 minutes.

Meanwhile, prepare the potatoes. Peel the potatoes, cut them in half lengthways, and then cut each half lengthways again into big wedges. Place a large pan over a medium heat. Pour in enough olive oil to cover the base of the pan. Once hot, gradually add in the potatoes. Do not add too many potatoes at once as this will lower the heat of the oil. Working in batches, cook the potatoes in a single layer for about 10 minutes until lightly golden, crisp on the outside and starting to soften on the inside. Transfer the potatoes to a plate lined with paper towels to drain. Season the potatoes with salt and pepper while still very hot.

After 40 minutes, remove and discard the cinnamon stick. One at a time, carefully nestle the fried potatoes in between the meat. Do not stir to avoid breaking the potatoes, instead shake the pan to mix. Cover with the lid slightly ajar and simmer for a further 40–50 minutes or until the sauce has thickened. Let the stew stand for 15 minutes, uncovered, before serving with the sauce.

Lachanodolmades **Stuffed cabbage rolls with an egg and lemon sauce**

FROM **SYROS AND TINOS**

SERVES 4–6

FOR THE CABBAGE ROLLS

- 1 very large or 2 smaller loose-leafed cabbages (around 3kg/6lb 12oz)
- 3 teaspoons salt
- 120g (4½oz) Carolina or arborio rice
- 250g (9oz) finely minced (ground) pork, ideally shoulder
- 250g (9oz) finely minced (ground) beef, ideally shoulder
- 1 carrot, peeled and grated (shredded)
- 1 large onion, peeled and grated (shredded)
- 2 spring onions (scallions), finely chopped (green parts reserved)
- 1 leek, finely chopped (green parts reserved)
- 1½ teaspoons dried mint
- 4 heaped tablespoons chopped parsley leaves (stems reserved)
- 3 tablespoons fennel fronds or dill, chopped (stems reserved)
- 3 tablespoons olive oil
- ½ teaspoon ground allspice (optional)
- 1½–2 teaspoons salt
- 1 teaspoon freshly ground black pepper

Traditionally prepared for Christmas and New Year, this dish is popular throughout winter across several islands, including Evia, Chios, Lesvos, Rhodes, Tinos, Corfu and Crete. Each island group has its own variation: for instance, in Rhodes, bulgur (cracked) wheat is used in the filling instead of rice and butter is added for flavour. On Syros, instead of the classic *avgolemono* (egg and lemon sauce, see page 91), cabbage rolls are drizzled with either a bechamel sauce or fusion of *avgolemono* and bechamel. In Crete, cabbage rolls are often vegan. Whether prepared with meat or not, they are served in a lemony broth rather than a sauce. On Corfu, where cabbage rolls are served during Easter, pancetta is added and tomato juice is incorporated in the sauce.

Historically, this recipe included only pork, closely tied to the cultural practice of *choirosfagia* (an ancient custom of pig butchery, see page 42). If you don't eat pork, use beef instead. Here, I combine elements from Corfiot and Cycladic cuisines. The filling includes meat, rice and herbs, and I add chunks of pancetta for extra flavour. When ready, I top the rolls with a delightful sauce similar to the one that is often enjoyed on Tinos or Syros. Wild fennel grows abundantly on most islands and is frequently used in local dishes. If wild fennel isn't available, dill works perfectly well as a substitute.

Wash the cabbage. Remove the thick, tough outer leaves and set them aside. Using a small paring knife, cut around the thick stem of the cabbage at the base, removing a conical section so that the leaves separate easily once boiled.

With the cut stem facing down, place the cabbage in a deep pan (it should fit comfortably). Fill the pan with enough water to cover two-thirds of the cabbage, add the salt and bring to a boil over a medium–high heat. Reduce the heat to medium and simmer for 15 minutes or until the leaves soften. To check if the cabbage leaves are ready, insert the tip of a knife into the centre of the cabbage from the stem side. It should easily pierce the heart of the cabbage. If the cabbage isn't soft all the way through, gently remove the softened outer leaves and continue boiling the rest for a further few minutes. Carefully transfer the cabbage to a colander, cut stem facing upwards, to drain and cool.

Soak the rice in cold water for 10 minutes. Drain in a sieve (strainer) and leave to dry. In a large bowl, combine the minced (ground) meat with the drained rice and remaining ingredients. Knead to mix well and season with salt and pepper.

To cook the cabbage rolls, place a wide, shallow pan over a medium–high heat. Add 1 tablespoon of the olive oil. Once hot, season the pancetta with salt and pepper, then add to the pan and sauté until brown all over. Leaving the oil in the pan, transfer the pancetta to a plate.

FOR COOKING THE CABBAGE ROLLS

150ml (5fl oz) olive oil
200g (7oz) pancetta, cut into small pieces
2–3 bay leaves
500ml (17fl oz) stock or water
Juice of ½ lemon

FOR THE SAUCE

2 tablespoons butter
2 tablespoons flour
2 egg yolks, at room temperature
Juice of 1 lemon (or more, depending on how lemony you like it)
½ teaspoon lemon zest
About 500ml (17fl oz) hot broth from the pot (if not enough, mix it with some chicken or beef stock)
Salt and freshly ground black pepper

Using the same pan, cover the base with the bay leaves, reserved green parts of the spring onions (scallions), leeks and herb stems. Arrange the tough outer cabbage leaves over the pan to create a secure base for the cabbage rolls.

Separate the cooked cabbage leaves. Using a sharp knife, cut away any parts with thick stems that aren't flexible. Cut any very large leaves into halves or quarters, use smaller leaves to patch any torn ones, or combine them with other leaves to wrap the rolls. If the inner leaves are tough, blanch them until softened.

Place a heaped tablespoon of filling on one of the cabbage leaves, then shape into an oblong patty that can be rolled in the leaf. (You may need to vary the amount of filling depending on the size of each leaf.) Fold both sides of the leaf inwards, then roll up, gently pressing to maintain its shape. Transfer the cabbage roll to the pan, seam side down to prevent it opening during cooking. Repeat to make more rolls, neatly placing them side by side in the pan. Once you have the first layer of cabbage rolls in the pan, tuck some pieces of pancetta into any gaps between them and season with a little salt and pepper. Continue to build a second layer of cabbage rolls until all the leaves and filling have been used. Tuck any remaining pancetta among the rolls and season again with salt and pepper.

Fill the pan with enough stock or water to reach, but not completely cover, the cabbage rolls. Pour in the remaining olive oil and lemon juice. Cover with an inverted plate to keep the rolls stable during cooking. Cook over a medium–low heat for 40–50 minutes, with the lid slightly ajar, until the filling is cooked and the liquid has reduced. Remove the pan from heat and let it cool for 10 minutes. Carefully remove the plate from the pot. Using a ladle, start to transfer the cooking liquid from the pan to a measuring jug (pitcher).

To make the sauce, melt the butter in a pan over a low heat. Add the flour and whisk continuously for 2 minutes to make a paste. Cook for 1–2 minutes, but do not let it brown. Gradually add two-thirds of the reserved hot stock, whisking continuously to avoid lumps. Continue cooking until the sauce thickens, about 5–7 minutes. Remove from heat and set aside for 2–3 minutes.

Put the egg yolks in a small bowl. While whisking vigorously, gradually add the lemon juice to the eggs until well combined. Mix in the zest. Temper the egg mixture by gradually adding the remaining hot stock while continuing to whisk. (Be careful at this point not to scramble the eggs.) Gradually add the egg and lemon mixture to the bechamel sauce, whisking continuously to combine. Return the pan to a low heat and continue cooking for a further 2–3 minutes or until the sauce is smooth and thickened. Season with salt and pepper to taste.

Place the cooked cabbage rolls on a platter and pour over the egg and lemon sauce. Garnish with fresh herbs, such as fennel fronds, dill or mint, if preferred. Serve the cabbage rolls warm with slices of good crusty bread.

Barbecue pork souvlaki with pita bread

FROM **THE ISLANDS**

MAKES 6

- 680g (1lb 8oz) pork neck or shoulder
- 2 tablespoons olive oil, plus extra for brushing the pita breads
- ¾ teaspoon dried oregano or chopped fresh parsley, plus extra for the pita breads
- ¾ teaspoon salt, plus extra for the pita breads

TO SERVE

- 6 pita breads (see page 17 for homemade)
- 1–2 tomatoes, halved and thinly sliced
- 1 small red onion, halved and thinly sliced
- Strained yogurt or tzatziki (see page 37, optional)
- Fried potatoes (optional)
- ½ teaspoon paprika (sweet or spicy, or a mix of both)

Souvlaki is the quintessential street food of Greece, eagerly devoured by tourists and locals alike. Enjoyed in various forms across all the islands, there's a misconception that souvlaki is made with lamb. In fact, the most popular version is with pork, chicken being the second favourite. Old-school souvlaki is my favourite. These are small in size and very simple, served either on the skewers with a wedge of lemon and sliced bread or wrapped in pita bread. When wrapped, they include only sliced tomatoes and onions, coarsely chopped parsley, some spicy paprika or just oregano. Often, a spoonful of tzatziki or plain yogurt is added in the wrap; I usually go for the latter as it balances best with the other flavours. These pork skewers are great when grilled on a barbecue, especially over charcoal, but they also work perfectly well in a griddle pan.

Some of my most cherished island memories are of evenings spent at open-air cinemas, a feature of many islands. These cinemas exude a vintage charm, enveloped by the fragrance of jasmine and basil. Tables are scattered among the seats, perfect for placing drinks and snacks. On these magical movie nights, we treat ourselves to souvlaki, paired with a cold beer, while watching a film under the twinkling island stars.

If using bamboo skewers, soak them in water for at least 30 minutes. If you are planning to barbecue the skewers, you may want to use metal skewers.

Remove the pork from the fridge 30 minutes before grilling to reach room temperature. Cut the meat into rough 2cm (¾ inch) cubes and place in a bowl. Add the olive oil, oregano and salt to the pork, mix well. Thread the meat onto the skewers, ensuring there is an equal amount on each one, then set aside.

Prepare the barbecue or place a griddle pan over medium–high heat. Once hot, grill the skewers for about 5 minutes or until browned on one side. Turn the skewers and cook on the other side until browned. Turn them onto the remaining uncooked two sides for about 1 minute each to ensure even cooking.

Meanwhile, grill the pita breads for a couple of minutes on each side. If there's enough space on the barbecue, place them alongside the skewers or you can place them on top of the meat for extra flavour. If you plan to use them as wraps, don't overcook them as they will dry out and break. Brush the pita breads with a little olive oil and sprinkle them lightly with dried oregano and salt.

Transfer the grilled souvlaki to a platter and serve with the pitas, either whole or quartered, if you're planning to wrap them. Serve the sliced tomatoes, onions, and yogurt or tzatziki on the side along with some fried potatoes. To wrap the souvlaki, remove the meat from the skewers and place it in the centre of a warm pita. Add 3 or 4 slices of tomato and onion on top. Dollop on some yogurt or tzatziki, sprinkle with a pinch of paprika and wrap it tightly. Neatly seal the wraps in food wrapping paper to keep them well-contained.

Pies & Pasties

CHAPTER 5

Kremidopita **Onion pie**

FROM **MYKONOS**

SERVES 8

FOR THE PASTRY

- 600g (1lb 5oz) plain (all-purpose) flour, plus extra for dusting
- ¾ teaspoon fine salt
- 125ml (4½fl oz) olive oil
- 3 tablespoons *tsipouro*, *raki*, vodka or grappa
- 1 tablespoon white wine vinegar
- 250ml (9fl oz) water, at room temperature

FOR THE FILLING

- 2 tablespoons olive oil
- 1 large onion, peeled and roughly chopped
- 1 leek, roughly chopped
- 8 spring onions (scallions), roughly chopped
- 1kg (2lb 4oz) *tyrovolia*, *anthotiro* or ricotta cheese
- Large handful of coarsely chopped spinach or chard leaves
- 6–7 tablespoons chopped fennel fronds or dill
- 3 eggs, lightly beaten
- Salt and freshly ground black pepper

The traditional cuisine of Mykonos stands in stark contrast to the cosmopolitan image the island exudes today. The challenges of cultivation on a very dry island made the livelihoods of Mykonians a tough endeavour, however, everything changed in the 1970s when the island was discovered by globetrotting elites. Despite the plethora of upscale restaurants that now dot the island, there are still hidden gems where one can uncover the essence of traditional local cuisine. Rooted in simplicity, these dishes rely on humble ingredients that were readily available to everyone.

There are locals on Mykonos who fight hard to preserve its traditions. I had the pleasure of meeting Irene Zouganeli, daughter of a Mykonian farmer and sister to the owner of Rizes – a project nestled in Maou, the old agricultural side of the island – which was set up on their ancestral farm with a mission to uphold local culture, spanning from the architectural aesthetics of village life to the culinary delights they cherish. Irene and her family are fervently committed to safeguarding the customs of old. She works as a private chef, channelling her passion for preserving and reviving the traditional Mykonian flavours she learnt from her mother and other local cooks.

Among local recipes, the iconic Mykonian onion pie is part of the island's culinary legacy. Crafted with accessible regional produce, including the creamy *tyrovolia* cheese and a medley of dried and fresh onions, Irene's rendition includes the addition of leeks, infusing the pie with a subtle sweetness. For extra flavour and moisture, she adds a handful of spinach or chard, as locals typically do. To elevate the dish further, Irene generously incorporates chopped fennel fronds or substitutes it with dill, when fennel is out of season. You could also use a combination of the two.

First, make the filo (phyllo) pastry. You can prepare the dough using either an electric stand mixer fitted with the hook attachment or knead it by hand. In the bowl of an electric stand mixer or a large mixing bowl, combine the flour and salt. Make a well in the centre of the flour and add the olive oil, *tsipouro*, vinegar and water, mixing all the liquids together in the bowl. Gradually incorporate the flour from the edges of the bowl into the wet ingredients while kneading at medium speed or using your hands until everything is incorporated. (You may need to slightly adjust the amount of flour due to the humidity.) The dough should be soft, smooth and elastic, but without sticking to your hands. Shape the dough into a ball, wrap it in cling film (plastic wrap) and leave to rest for 30 minutes.

Meanwhile, prepare the filling. Place a large, deep pan over a medium heat and add the oil. Once hot, add the onion, leek and spring onions to the pan and sauté until golden. Season with salt and pepper, then remove the pan from heat.

Recipe continues overleaf

In a large mixing bowl, mash the *tyrovolia, anthotiro* or ricotta using a large fork or potato masher. Stir in the sautéed onions and leek along with the spinach or chard, if using, the fennel fronds or dill until well combined. Taste and adjust the seasoning with salt and freshly ground black pepper. Finally, mix in the eggs.

Preheat the oven to 190°C/170°C/375°F/gas 5. Oil a 38cm (15 inch) round baking pan or ovenproof dish.

Dust a large work surface with flour and keep some extra flour to hand nearby. Divide the dough into two equal parts and shape into balls. Keep the second ball covered with a clean dish towel to prevent it drying out. Place the first ball on the floured surface and press down to form a flat disk. Dust the dough with a little flour and, using a long, narrow rolling pin, start rolling it out, keeping the circular shape. The dough is quite elastic, so you can stretch it further by hand, being careful not to tear it – this filo pastry can be rolled slightly thicker than regular filo. Roll out into a disk slightly larger than the pan or dish. (The excess pastry will hang over the rim and then be used to seal the pie.)

Roll the pastry around the rolling pin, then transfer the sheet to the prepared pan, gently unrolling it so that it evenly covers the surface of the pan and the excess filo hangs over the rim. Spoon the pie filling on top of the pastry and spread it evenly using a spatula.

Roll out the second ball of dough in the same way as the first and place it on top of the filling. Twist any excess filo pastry up and inwards, working all the way round to seal the pie and form a rim. Using a toothpick, make small holes over the surface of the pie. Using a paring knife, score the pie into portions. (I score it into triangular pieces, like a pizza, but it can be scored into squares.) Brush the pastry generously with olive oil. Spray the pie with water to achieve a crisp crust.

Place the pie on the bottom rack of the hot oven and bake for about 1 hour, or until the pastry is golden on top. (If the pastry is golden before the end of the cooking time, place a piece of parchment paper over the top.) Leave the pie to cool for 20–30 minutes before slicing and serving. The pie can be served either warm or at room temperature.

NOTE

Instead of filo (phyllo) pastry, you can use ready-rolled puff pastry. Simply lay one large sheet of puff pastry in the base of the pan and then lay another sheet on top of the pie filling. (It might make two pies if the puff pastry sheets are relatively small.) Before baking, brush the pastry with egg wash or olive oil to achieve a golden finish. When made with puff pastry, the pie will require less time to bake, about 35–40 minutes or until golden.

Ladenia **Smoky aubergine, tomato and feta pie**

FROM **KIMOLOS**

SERVES 4

FOR THE BASE

500g (1lb 2oz) plain (all-purpose) flour
¾ teaspoon salt
4g (1 teaspoon) dried yeast
1 teaspoon sugar
250ml (9fl oz) lukewarm water
1 tablespoon olive oil, plus a bit extra for oiling the bowl and dough

FOR THE TOPPING

2 small aubergines (eggplants, around 350g/12½oz)
250g (9oz) cherry tomatoes, quartered and deseeded
1 red onion, cut into quarters and thinly sliced
2 teaspoons dried oregano
80ml (2½fl oz) olive oil, plus 20ml (⅔fl oz) for oiling the pan
20–30g (¾–1oz) feta, crumbled
Sea salt and freshly ground black pepper

TO SERVE

1 heaped tablespoon capers, rinsed and dried
1 tablespoon chopped fresh parsley

Kimolos is a true paradise. This enchanting volcanic island, nestled beside Milos in the Aegean, has given me some of the best swims of my life. Historically, Kimolos was celebrated for its high-quality chalk, known in Greek as *kimolia*, which was mined and exported, lending the island its name. Renowned for its tranquil landscapes, pristine beaches and turquoise waters, Kimolos features a rugged terrain with its main village perched on a hill. This village, a maze of narrow streets and whitewashed houses, is one of the finest examples of fortified architecture in the Aegean, blending seamlessly with the island's natural beauty, while the northern part of the island remains untouched and protected, serving as a sanctuary for the Mediterranean monk seal.

Kimolos's cuisine is a celebration of seafood, complemented by its renowned cheese production. The island is also famous for its baked goods, such as breads, rusks and various pies. Among these, Ladenia stands out with its Venetian roots, resembling a thick-crusted pizza or focaccia. The classic version is topped with sliced tomatoes, onions, capers and oregano, but – like pizza – it invites endless variations. My personal take here includes smoky aubergines and feta, a delightful combination that perfectly captures the essence of a Greek summer.

First, make the base. You can prepare the dough using either an electric stand mixer fitted with the hook attachment or knead it by hand. In the bowl of an electric stand mixer or a large mixing bowl, combine the flour and salt. In a separate larger bowl, combine the yeast with the sugar and water. Make a well in the centre of the flour and add the olive oil and yeast mixture. Gradually incorporate the flour from the edges of the bowl into the wet ingredients while kneading at medium speed or using your hands until everything is incorporated. (You may need to slightly adjust the amount of flour.) Knead the dough for 10 minutes by hand or for 5 minutes in a stand mixer fitted with the hook attachment. The dough should be soft, smooth and elastic. Shape the dough into a ball, grease the bowl and dough with a little olive oil, return the dough to the bowl and cover with a clean dish towel. Leave the dough to rise for about 1 hour 30 minutes or until it doubles in size.

Meanwhile, prepare the topping. Preheat the grill (broiler) to 200°C/400°F or prepare the barbecue if cooking over an open flame. Prick the aubergines all over with a fork and place them on a baking tray. Grill the aubergines for 15 minutes or until soft, then turn them over and grill for a further 15 minutes or until very soft, shrivelled and charred. Set aside to cool. Once cool enough to handle, scoop out the flesh into a colander and discard the skins and seeds. Season with a little salt and set aside.

Place the tomatoes in a separate colander, season them with a little salt and set aside to drain.

When the dough is ready, preheat the oven to 200°C/180°C fan/400°F/gas 6 and generously oil a 30–35cm (12–14-inch) deep baking pan or ovenproof dish. Place the dough in the centre of the pan or dish and, using your fingers, spread it out until it reaches the edges.

Lay the red onion slices over the surface of the dough and sprinkle with salt. Next, arrange the quartered tomatoes on top and sprinkle with the dried oregano and season with freshly ground black pepper. Drizzle with 50ml (1¾fl oz) of the remaining olive oil. Bake on the middle rack of the hot oven for 25–30 minutes or until the crust is crispy and golden.

Remove the pie from the oven and shred the grilled aubergine over the top. Drizzle with the remaining 30ml (1fl oz) of olive oil and season with freshly ground black pepper. Crumble the feta on top of the pie and return to the oven for a further 10–15 minutes or until the feta has softened and the pie crust is golden and crispy around the edges.

Sprinkle the capers and chopped parsley over the pie before slicing and serving.

THE ISLAND COOPERATIVES

Island cooperatives, or co-ops, are more than just economic entities; they are the beating heart of many Greek islands, weaving together the social and cultural fabric of their communities. These co-ops foster a sense of unity, preserve time-honoured traditions, and promote local products, making them indispensable to both cultural heritage and economic sustainability.

On these units, artisans, farmers, producers or local women, showcase their creations, each item telling a story of tradition and craftsmanship.

Agricultural co-ops help farmers pool their resources to cultivate and market local gems such as cheeses and other dairy products, olive oil and olives, like the famous Throuba olives from Thasos, and renown local island produce such the Chios mastiha or the Zante currants. These co-ops ensure that the quality and authenticity of these products remain uncompromised, all while promoting sustainable farming practices.

Artisanal co-ops play an equally vital role. On islands such as Sifnos and Rhodes, known for their exquisite ceramics, co-ops support local potters in bringing their beautifully crafted wares to a broader audience, both locally and internationally. Similar co-ops on Crete focus on textiles, including rugs, blankets and clothing. Crafted using traditional looms and techniques, these items often feature beautiful patterns and vibrant colours, each piece a testament to the island's rich cultural heritage.

Many Greek islands boast notable co-ops focused on their renowned wines, such as Santo Wines on Santorini or the Samos Wine Cooperative, which supports local vineyards in producing sweet Muscat wines, preserving the island's traditional wine-making practices.

On Ikaria, a women's cooperative in Raches produces traditional foods like sweet preserves, jams (preserves), herbal tea blends and liqueurs. In Lesvos, the women's co-op in Mesotopos is one of the most well-organised and profitable island co-ops. The women there create a wide array of wonderful local delicacies, including baked goods, traditional desserts and the famous local hahles. Hahles is a product made of wheat boiled in fermented milk (traditional trahanas), formed into a dough, shaped into cups and sun-dried. They can be enjoyed in many ways, most often as rusks, plain or stuffed with cheese and tomatoes and baked, or traditionally grilled over charcoal and then dipped in wine.

These co-ops do more than support local economies; they are guardians of tradition, they empower farmers or local women and they preserve traditional production methods and recipes, ensuring that cultural heritage is maintained for future generations. Community involvement is at the core of co-ops, fostering a sense of collective identity and pride.

Pitia **Pasties with spinach, greens and fresh herbs**

FROM **KARPATHOS**

MAKES 10–12

FOR THE PASTRY
4g (1 teaspoon) dried yeast
200ml (7fl oz) lukewarm water
500g (1lb 2oz) plain (all-purpose) flour
½ teaspoon salt
100ml (3½fl oz) olive oil

FOR THE FILLING
400g (14oz) fresh spinach, trimmed and coarsely chopped
200g (7oz) chard, trimmed and coarsely chopped
¾–1 teaspoon salt
5–6 spring onions (scallions), chopped (green part too if fresh)
1 small onion, finely chopped
100g (3½oz) courgette (zucchini), coarsely grated (shredded)
1 firm tomato (around 100g/3½oz), cored, deseeded and diced
50g (1¾oz) Carolina or arborio rice (or use bulgur or cracked wheat)
3–4 tablespoons chopped dill or fennel fronds
Salt and freshly ground black pepper
Olive oil, for brushing

I was given this recipe by Gina Moschonas, the mother of two dear friends of mine, Fani and George Maltas from Karpathos. Though Fani and George spent most of their childhood on Rhodes, being close to Karpathos meant they frequently sailed over to visit their grandmother and her sisters. It was about 16 years ago, during Easter, when Fani and George first introduced me to their island. That trip left a lasting impression on me; the warmth of the people, the delightful foods and the incredible hospitality will always hold a special place in my heart. In Mesohori, a communal wood-burning oven was a central part of the village's weekly routine. Every Saturday, locals would typically knead their weekly bread, then transport it to the communal oven for baking. By early noon, the breads and pasties would be loaded onto donkeys, still warm from the oven, and brought home for a delicious lunch.

Fani fondly recalls the Saturdays spent with her grandmother and aunts, as they baked bread for the entire week ahead. They would roll out the same dough into a thicker filo (phyllo) to make *pitia* or *lachanopitia*, as they call them in the island's southern villages. These delightful yet simple pasties are filled with seasonal greens or vegetables from their gardens. The filo pastry used for these pasties is slightly thicker as it contains yeast. Despite their simplicity, these pasties are incredibly flavourful and are traditionally served with a spicy local cheese on the side. They make a perfect starter to share before a main meal or can even be enjoyed in place of bread.

First, make the pastry. In a small bowl, combine the yeast with 40ml (1⅓fl oz) of the lukewarm water. Let it stand for 5 minutes. In the bowl of an electric stand mixer fitted with the hook attachment, mix together the flour and salt. Make a well in the centre of the flour, then pour in the yeast mixture, olive oil and the remaining lukewarm water. Mix at medium speed until the dough is soft, smooth and elastic. (You may need to add a little extra water, but only add it 1 teaspoon at a time until you reach the correct consistency.) Shape the dough into a ball, place into a large bowl and cover with a clean dish towel. Let the dough rise for about 1 hour or until it doubles in size.

Meanwhile, prepare the filling. Place spinach and chard in a large mixing bowl, add ¾ teaspoon salt and knead relatively hard, as though you are kneading dough, until they reduce in volume. (If your hands are sensitive, wear gloves for this.) Drain off any excess water, then transfer the spinach and chard to a colander along with the spring onions, courgette and tomato. Set aside to drain until the dough is ready to roll out.

Recipe continues overleaf

In a large tray or bowl, mix together the greens and dill or fennel fronds. Season with salt and freshly ground black pepper if necessary.

Preheat the oven to 180°C/160°C/350°F/gas 4. Line two baking trays with parchment paper.

Dust a large work surface with flour and keep some extra flour to hand nearby. Divide the dough into small pieces, each weighing about 60–70g (2–2½oz) depending on your preferred size of pasties, and shape into balls. Working one at a time, press down each ball and roll it out into a small disk about 15–17cm (6–7 inches) in diameter. Pile 2–3 heaped tablespoonfuls of the filling into the centre of each disk and, using the back of the spoon, spread it out over the pastry surface while leaving a clear border around the edges. (Any leftover filling can be stored in the freezer for up to 6 months.)

Brush a little water around the edges of the pastry, then fold the pastry disks over into half-moons. There is a traditional way to seal these pasties; you can either pinch, lift, and twist the pastry to create a decorative seal or simply use a fork to press along the open side for a secure closure. Arrange the prepared pasties on the lined baking trays, then brush them generously with olive oil for a golden finish.

Bake on the bottom rack of the hot oven for about 45 minutes or until the pastry turns light golden brown.

Tourtes **Cheese and mint pasties**

FROM **SYMI**

MAKES 15–18

FOR THE FILO (PHYLLO) PASTRY

- 1 teaspoon ground *mastiha* (optional)
- Pinch of sugar (optional)
- 125g (4½oz) butter
- 200g (7oz) strained Greek-style yogurt
- 135ml (4¾fl oz) whole (full-fat) milk
- 1 egg
- 500g (1lb 2oz) plain (all-purpose) flour, plus extra for dusting
- ½ teaspoon baking powder
- ¼ teaspoon salt

FOR THE FILLING

- 350g (12½oz) *anthotyro* or ricotta
- 80g (2½oz) feta (vegetarian, if needed)
- 200g (7oz) hard yellow cheese (such as *kefalotyri*, regato or pecorino), grated (shredded)
- 2 eggs
- 1 tablespoon flour
- ½ teaspoon baking powder
- ½ tablespoon dried mint or 1½ tablespoons chopped fresh mint
- Salt and freshly ground black pepper

Charming pastel-coloured houses, boasting tiled roofs and graceful facades, give the island an allure. One of its notable landmarks is the eighteenth-century Panormitis Monastery, dedicated to the Archangel Michael, revered as the patron not only of Symi but of sailors across the Dodecanese. A unique tradition associated with the monastery involves sailors inscribing their prayers, sealing them in bottles and casting them into the sea, believing they would reach the monastery by a wind-sheltered bay. The museum at the monastery exhibits many of these recovered bottles.

Nestled within the grounds of the Panormitis Monastery lies the Panormitis Bakery, an enchanting establishment renowned for its freshly baked local delicacies. Among its offerings are the traditional ring-shaped rusks, hung from the ceiling for drying and serving as decorative elements. A highlight is the local cheese pasties known as *tourtes*, typically prepared during Easter. This delectable recipe features a pastry made with yogurt, eggs and a hint of chios mastiha for flavour, although it can be omitted. The filling, a blend of various cheeses infused with chopped mint, is central to this culinary delight.

First, make the pastry. If using pieces of *mastiha*, place 3 or 4 'tears' in the freezer for around 1 hour until hardened. Once hard, using a pestle and mortar, grind the *mastiha* with a pinch of sugar into a fine powder. Next, melt butter in a small saucepan over a low heat. If you're using *mastiha*, stir it into the melted butter. Remove the pan from the heat and allow the mixture to cool for a few minutes. In a mixing bowl, thoroughly mix together the yogurt with the milk and egg.

In the bowl of an electric stand mixer fitted with the hook attachment, combine the flour, baking powder and salt. Create a well in the centre of the flour and pour in the yogurt mixture and cooled melted butter. Mix at medium speed for about 3 minutes or until a soft, smooth and elastic dough forms. The dough should roll out easily without being sticky. Cover the bowl with a clean dish towel and let it rest for 30 minutes.

Meanwhile, prepare the filling. Place the *anthotyro* or ricotta in a large mixing bowl and mash it well with a fork or potato masher. Crumble in the feta and repeat the mashing process. Next, add the grated (shredded) hard cheese and mix thoroughly to combine.

In a separate bowl, beat the eggs until frothy and then pour them into the cheese mixture. Add the flour, baking powder, dried or fresh mint and mix well to combine. Season well with salt and freshly ground black pepper to taste.

Recipe continues overleaf

Preheat the oven to 190°C/170°C fan/375°F/gas 5 and line a baking tray with parchment paper.

Dust a large work surface with flour and keep some extra flour to hand nearby. Divide the dough into small pieces, each weighing about 60–70g (2–2½oz) depending on your preferred size of pasties, and shape into balls. Working one at a time, press down each ball and roll it out into a small disk about 13–15cm (5–6 inches) in diameter. Pile 2–3 heaped tablespoonfuls of the filling into the centre of each disk and, using the back of the spoon, spread it out over the pastry surface while leaving a clear border around the edges. Fold the pastry disks over into half-moons and use a fork to press around the edges to seal the pasties well and create a decorative pattern. Place the pasties on the prepared baking tray.

Bake the pasties on the bottom rack of the hot oven for 30–35 minutes or until golden brown. Remove from the oven and leave to cool slightly – the cheese filling will be very hot. These can be eaten cold but they are best enjoyed when still slightly warm.

Bakalaopita **Cod pie**

FROM **KEFALONIA**

SERVES 8

FOR THE PASTRY

550g (1lb 4oz) plain (all-purpose) flour, plus extra for dusting
¾ teaspoon fine salt
120ml (4½fl oz) olive oil
120ml (4½fl oz) dry white wine
50–75ml (1¾–2½fl oz) lukewarm water

FOR THE FILLING

850g (1lb 4oz) cod fillets (either fresh or frozen and defrosted)
100g (3½oz) Carolina or arborio rice
430g (15oz) ripe cherry tomatoes
2 tablespoons olive oil
190g (7oz) chopped onion
80g (2½oz) courgette (zucchini), coarsely grated (shredded)
2 garlic cloves, peeled and roughly chopped
70ml (2½fl oz) dry rosé or white wine
¼ teaspoon ground cinnamon
¼ teaspoon ground allspice
¼ teaspoon orange zest (unwaxed)
6 tablespoons chopped parsley
1½ tablespoons chopped marjoram or 1 teaspoon dried marjoram
Salt and freshly ground black pepper

TO FINISH

2–3 tablespoons sesame seeds
1 tablespoon nigella seeds

Kefalonia, the largest of the Ionian Islands, is famed for its varied and captivating landscapes, encompassing rugged mountains, lush valleys and pristine shorelines. Among its notable features is Mount Ainos, the tallest peak in the Ionian archipelago, offering awe-inspiring vistas of the surrounding terrain. The island boasts a rich culinary tradition, reflecting its Mediterranean setting and diverse historical influences from civilizations such as the Venetians, Byzantines and British.

Among the island's culinary treasures are two renowned recipes: the local meat pie and Bakalaopita, a pie traditionally crafted with salted cod – a staple ingredient in historic Venetian cuisine. Personally, I prefer to prepare this pie with fresh cod, a tip passed down to me by my mother's dear friend, Kiki Sereti, who hails from Kefalonia. The pie filling is infused with cinnamon, allspice, orange zest and wild marjoram, imparting a delightful aroma and masking any fishy odours.

Filo (phyllo) pastry on the island is typically made with wine, lending it a crisp and dry texture. This variety of filo is particularly well-suited for indulgent fillings such as fish, meat or creamy mushroom pies. With a single layer on the bottom and top, this filo is thicker, avoiding any greasiness while providing a flavourful and crunchy crust.

First, make the filo pastry. You can prepare the dough using either an electric stand mixer fitted with the hook attachment or kneading it by hand. In the bowl of a stand mixer or a large mixing bowl, combine the flour and salt. Create a well in the centre of the flour and pour in the olive oil, wine and 4 tablespoons of water. Begin mixing with a spatula until the wet ingredients are incorporated into the flour, forming a dough. (If using a stand mixer, mix at medium speed.) Gradually add extra water as needed, one tablespoon at a time, until you have a soft, smooth and elastic dough. Shape the dough into a ball, wrap it in cling film (plastic wrap), and let it rest for 30 minutes.

Meanwhile, prepare the filling. Bring about 1 litre (34fl oz) of water to a boil in a large pan. Season the water with plenty of salt and gently lower the cod fillets into the boiling water. Reduce the heat to medium-low and simmer the fish for about 10 minutes or until they are fully cooked. Once cooked, strain the fish and reserve the cooking liquid. Place the cooked fish in a bowl and use a fork to shred it. Combine the shredded fish with 2–3 tablespoons of the reserved cooking liquid and set aside.

Rinse the rice. Puree the tomatoes in a food processor. Set both aside.

Heat the olive oil in a large, deep pan over a medium heat. Add the onions and sauté until softened, then add the courgette and garlic. Season with salt and pepper and cook until the vegetables have softened and most of the liquid has evaporated. Add the rinsed rice, followed by the shredded cod, and sauté for 1 minute. Pour in the wine and let everything simmer until the alcohol evaporates slightly. Next, add the puréed tomatoes, season with salt and pepper, then simmer gently for 3–4 minutes until the mixture is juicy but not too dry. Allow the filling to cool slightly, then adjust the seasoning as necessary. Once cooled, mix in about 4–5 tablespoons of the fish cooking liquid to moisten the filling. The exact amount needed will vary depending on the moisture level of the filling; aim for a juicy consistency without being soupy, as this will affect the filo pastry.

Preheat the oven to 190°C/170°C fan/375°F/gas 5. Oil a 35cm (14-inch) round, deep baking pan or ovenproof dish.

Dust a large work surface with flour and keep some extra flour to hand nearby. Divide the dough into two equal parts and shape into balls. Keep the second ball covered with a clean cloth to prevent it drying out. Place the first ball on the floured surface and press down to form a flat disk. Dust the dough with a little flour and, using a long, narrow rolling pin, start rolling it out, keeping the circular shape. Roll out into a relatively thin sheet that is slightly larger than the pan or dish. (This excess pastry will hang over the rim and then be used to seal the pie.)

Roll the filo pastry around the rolling pin, then transfer the sheet to the prepared pan, gently unrolling it so that it evenly covers the surface of the pan and the excess pastry hangs over the rim. Spoon the pie filling on top of the pastry and spread it evenly using a spatula.

Roll out the second ball of dough in the same way as the first and place it on top of the filling. Twist any excess filo pastry up and inwards, working all the way around to seal the pie and form a rim. Using a toothpick, make small holes over the surface of the pie. Using a paring knife, score the pie into portions. (Score it into triangular pieces, like a pizza, or into squares.) Brush the pastry generously with olive oil and sprinkle over the sesame and nigella seeds. Spray the pie with water to achieve a crisp crust.

Place the pie on the bottom rack of the hot oven and bake for about 1 hour, or until the pastry is golden on top. Leave the pie to cool for 20–30 minutes before slicing and serving.

NOTE

Instead of filo (phyllo) pastry, you can use ready-rolled puff pastry. Simply lay one large sheet in the base of the pan and then lay another sheet on top of the pie filling. (If the puff pastry sheets are relatively small, make two pies instead.) Before baking, brush the pastry with egg wash or olive oil for a golden finish.

Grains & Pulses

CHAPTER 6

Tsouvras **Tomato soup with rice**

FROM **TILOS**

SERVES 4

70g (2½oz) short-grained white rice
1kg (2lb 4oz) ripe tomatoes
70ml (2½fl oz) olive oil
1 onion, peeled and finely chopped
1 garlic clove, peeled and minced
2–3 fresh thyme springs
1 bay leaf
1 whole dried red chilli or fresh red chilli (optional)
Pinch of sugar (optional, if the tomatoes are too sour)
1 heaped teaspoon tomato paste (concentrated purée)
800ml–1 litre (27–34fl oz) hot vegetable stock
Salt and freshly ground black pepper

TO SERVE
2–3 tablespoons strained Greek-style yogurt
2 tablespoons chopped toasted pine nuts
2 tablespoons chopped basil
Olive oil

Comforting yet quick to prepare, this tasty soup hails from Tilos, a small mountainous island that is part of the Dodecanese, nestled between Rhodes and Kos. Tilos is known for its absolute tranquillity, with serene surroundings, beautiful white-washed houses and narrow alleys just wide enough for a person to pass through.

Known locally as *tsouvras*, this soup is traditionally made with rice, bulgur (cracked) wheat or *trahanas*, but it can also be prepared with quinoa or any small pasta. I enjoy topping it with a little yogurt, some chopped basil and a handful of pine nuts for added flavour. (For a vegan version, use a plant-based Greek-style yogurt or omit it altogether.) This soup can be enjoyed either hot or chilled. I love it served with toasted garlic bread on the side.

Rinse the rice under cold running water, then drain in a colander and set aside to dry.

Blanch the tomatoes in hot water, then remove the skins and seeds. Place the tomato flesh in a food processor and blend until smooth. You should have about 800–850ml (27–29fl oz) of tomato purée. If necessary, blanch and blend a few more tomatoes to reach this quantity. Set aside.

Heat the olive oil in a large pan with a lid over a medium heat. Once hot, add the onion with a pinch of salt and sauté, stirring continuously, until the onions soften. Add the garlic, thyme, bay leaf, whole dried or fresh chilli and sugar (if using), then stir for a further 1 minute. Stir the tomato paste into the other ingredients in the pan.

Pour the reserved tomato purée into the pan along with 800ml (27fl oz) of the hot vegetable stock. Season with salt and black pepper to taste. Cover then pan with the lid and bring the contents to a simmer. Once simmering, reduce the heat and let everything cook gently, covered, for about 25–30 minutes, adding more stock if needed.

Remove and discard the thyme sprigs, bay leaf and chilli. Using a handheld stick (immersion) blender, blitz the soup in the pan until smooth. Taste the soup and adjust the seasoning, if necessary. Add the rice to the pan and cook the soup over a low heat for a further 10–15 minutes or until the rice is cooked.

Ladle the soup into deep bowls and serve topped with 1 or 2 teaspoons of Greek yogurt, a few toasted pine nuts, some chopped basil, a drizzle of olive oil and plenty of black pepper.

NOTE
Avoid storing fresh tomatoes in the fridge as they lose their texture and juices, and never ripen properly. Let them ripen at room temperature, stem side up. If you can't find juicy fresh tomatoes, opt for high-quality jarred or canned ones.

Fakes ardistes **Lentil soup with small pasta**

FROM **ASTYPALEA**

SERVES 6

400g (14oz) brown lentils
180ml (6fl oz) olive oil
1 large onion, peeled and grated (shredded)
1 carrot, peeled and grated (shredded)
3 garlic cloves, peeled and minced
1 tablespoon tomato paste (concentrated purée)
2 bay leaves
1 fresh thyme spring
270g (10oz) ripe tomatoes, grated (shredded) or use store-bought passata (strained tomatoes)
2.3–2.5 litres (78–84fl oz) hot water
130g (4½oz) semi di melone pasta (or orzo or any other small star-shaped pasta)
3–4 tablespoons chopped fresh mint
Salt and freshly ground black pepper

FOR THE ONIONS

3 tablespoons olive oil
2 large onions, peeled, halved and thinly sliced
1 fresh thyme spring
3 tablespoons red wine vinegar
Salt and freshly ground black pepper

Located on the westernmost point of the Dodecanese, Astypalea is known as the 'Butterfly of the Aegean' due to the island's distinctive shape, with a narrow isthmus connecting two larger landmasses. Astypalea uniquely combines elements of both the Cyclades and the Dodecanese, offering a blend of stunning landscapes and traditional architecture. The main town is built like an amphitheatre, with whitewashed houses climbing the hill up to the Venetian Castle of Kouerini. At the centre of the town, eight windmills stand in a line. In recent years, Astypalea has gained attention for its sustainability efforts, becoming a model for eco-friendly tourism.

Among my preferred Astypalea dishes is this lentil soup featuring locally crafted, small pasta called *ardista*. I usually opt for a store-bought alternative such as semi di melone or orzo. This is a wholesome meal relished by my son Apollo. For a full Greek experience, serve this soup with juicy olives, salted sardines and some good bread.

First, prepare the onions. Heat the oil in a large pan over a medium-high heat. Add the sliced onions to the pan along with the thyme and a pinch of salt and sauté, stirring continuously, until the onions have softened completely. Mix the vinegar into the onions and stir for a further few minutes or until the vinegar has been fully absorbed. Remove and discard the thyme, then season the onions with salt and pepper to taste. Set aside.

Rinse the lentils under cold running water, then drain in a colander and set aside to dry.

Heat 4 tablespoons of the olive oil in a large pan with a lid over a medium-high heat. Once hot, add the grated (shredded) onion and carrot with a pinch of salt and sauté, stirring continuously, until the onion softens. Add the garlic and tomato paste, then stir to mix well. Add the bay leaves, thyme and grated tomato.

Pour 2.3 litres (78fl oz) of hot water into the pan, then season with salt and pepper. Reduce the heat to medium-low, cover the pan with a lid and gently simmer for 30 minutes or until the lentils are al dente. Add the remaining olive oil to the pan, cover again and continue to simmer for a further 10–15 minutes or until the lentils are soft. Check occasionally and top up with more water if needed – the soup needs to be quite thin and watery before the pasta is added.

Once the lentils are cooked, add the pasta and cook in the broth for the time stated in the packet instructions (typically 8–10 minutes) or until tender. Remove the pan from heat, stir through the reserved cooked onions and the chopped mint. Season the soup with plenty of black pepper before serving.

Melitzanorizo **Aubergine rice**

FROM **CHIOS AND SYROS**

SERVES 4

- 350g (12½oz) Carolina or arborio rice
- 2 aubergines (eggplants, about 650g/1lb 7oz)
- 120ml (4fl oz) olive oil
- 2 onions, peeled and finely chopped
- 2 bay leaves
- 4–5 allspice berries
- 3 garlic cloves, peeled and finely chopped
- 550g (1lb 4oz) fresh ripe tomatoes, grated (shredded)
- 1 Romano pepper, deseeded and diced
- 500ml (17fl oz) hot vegetable stock (or you can use hot water)
- 2–3 heaped tablespoons chopped fresh parsley
- 2–3 heaped tablespoons chopped fresh mint
- Salt and freshly ground black pepper
- Lemon wedges, to serve (optional)

During aubergine (eggplant) season, this summertime rice dish is a staple on both Chios and Syros, two islands that were major centres of trade and culture. Despite their geographical separation, they share a rich historical connection as several people from Chios and the nearby island of Psara relocated to Syros in the early 1820s. Later, Greeks from Smyrna and the Turkish coast also moved there. This cultural exchange is reflected in the local cuisine.

This humble risotto-style dish showcases the fusion of aubergine and tomatoes, which meld beautifully into the rice. Stirring through chopped parsley at the end adds a burst of freshness. In Chios, they elevate the dish further by incorporating chopped mint, a touch that I particularly enjoy. Feel free to experiment with different varieties of rice, adjusting the quantity of broth and cooking time accordingly.

Rinse the rice under cold running water, then drain in a colander and set aside to dry.

Slice the stems from the aubergines, then peel and halve them. Place the aubergines in a heatproof bowl, cover them with warm water, add a pinch of salt and leave them to soak for 30 minutes. Once soaked, drain the aubergines, pat them dry and cut into rough 1cm (½ inch) cubes.

Heat 100ml (3½fl oz) of the olive oil in a pan with a lid over a medium heat. Add the aubergines along with the onions, bay leaves and allspice berries and sauté until the aubergines are golden. Add the garlic, toss everything together for 1 minute, then add the rice. Stir everything well to coat the grains of rice in the oil. Add the grated tomato and diced Romano pepper and cook while stirring for 2–3 minutes.

Pour in about 100ml (3½fl oz) of the stock and cook while stirring. Once the rice has absorbed most of the stock but is not completely dry, add some more stock and cook while continuing to stir. Repeat until all the remaining stock has been added, then let everything gently simmer, shaking the pan and stirring occasionally. This typically takes about 20 minutes.

When the rice is almost cooked, remove and discard the bay leaves and, if you prefer, the allspice berries too. Stir through the parsley and mint and any remaining olive oil, then gently simmer the rice over a very low heat for 2–3 minutes while stirring continuously. Remove the pan from the heat. Cover the top of the pan with a clean dish towel and place the lid on top. Let the rice rest for a few minutes before serving. If preferred, you can squeeze over a little lemon juice.

Revithia me melintzanes **Baked chickpeas with aubergines**

VE GF

FROM **PATMOS**

SERVES 4

FOR THE CHICKPEAS

300g (10½oz) dried chickpeas (garbanzo beans) or 650g (1lb 7oz) cooked chickpeas
1 bay leaf

FOR THE AUBERGINES

3 aubergines (eggplants, around 750g/17oz)
Olive oil, for brushing

FOR THE SAUCE

200ml (7fl oz) olive oil
1 onion, peeled and chopped
3 garlic cloves, peeled and roughly chopped
1 red bell pepper, deseeded and roughly chopped
1 bay leaf
1 tablespoon tomato paste (concentrated purée)
70ml (2½fl oz) sweet red wine
360g (13oz) fresh tomatoes, grated (shredded) or passata (strained tomatoes)
1 cinnamon stick
1 teaspoon sweet paprika
4 whole allspice berries
½ teaspoon grated orange zest (unwaxed)
3–4 fresh thyme sprigs
1 dried red chilli or fresh red chilli
400ml (14fl oz) warm vegetable broth or water
2–3 tablespoons finely chopped fresh parsley
Salt and freshly ground black pepper

Chickpeas (garbanzo beans) are a staple on Greek islands, particularly in the Cyclades, Dodecanese and on Crete, where they feature prominently in local recipes. These dishes often involve slow-cooking the chickpeas in a clay pot with a fitted lid, sealed with dough, to trap steam inside. The pot is placed in a wood-burning oven for hours. Baked chickpeas are a popular dish for island festivals, such as those on Nisyros and Sifnos. Variations on oven-baked chickpeas can be found across the islands, cooked with seasonal vegetables, fish or meat. In Rhodes, a dish called *lakani* features goat with bulgur (cracked) wheat and chickpeas. On Crete, chickpeas are paired with salted cod, while on Patmos, they are cooked with aubergines (eggplants).

On Patmos, the site of several important religious festivals, including the Feast Day of Saint John, this dish is typically cooked on the stove top with diced aubergines that melt into the tomato sauce with the chickpeas, creating a creamy texture. However, I prefer to bake the dish and halve or quarter the aubergines because this method allows them to retain their shape and absorb the flavours more distinctly. The baking process intensifies the flavours, giving the chickpeas a deeper, richer taste while the aubergines add a satisfying textural contrast.

If using dried chickpeas, place them in a large bowl, cover with plenty of water and leave to soak overnight. The next day, drain the chickpeas and place them in a pot covered in plenty of fresh water. Add a bay leaf and a little salt to the pot, then boil the chickpeas for about 40 minutes (depending on their quality) or until soft. Once cooked, drain the chickpeas and set aside.

Rinse the aubergines and pat them dry. Trim the leaves around the stem, but leaving the stem in place, and halve or quarter the aubergines lengthwise. Put the aubergines in a large bowl, add 1 teaspoon of salt and toss to coat. Cover the aubergines with lukewarm water and place a plate on top of them to keep them submerged in the water. Leave them to soak for 20–30 minutes, then drain and press the aubergines between kitchen paper to dry them well.

Preheat the oven to 200°C/180°C fan/400°F/gas 6. Line a baking tray with parchment paper.

Using a paring knife, score the flesh of the aubergines on both sides with vertical and horizontal lines to create a grid, then brush them generously with olive oil and season with salt and black pepper. Arrange the aubergines on the baking tray, cut sides up. Roast in the hot oven for 25 minutes or until soft and golden.

Recipe continues overleaf

Meanwhile, make the sauce. Place a large, deep pan over a medium heat. Add 50ml (1¾fl oz) of the olive oil and, once hot, tip in the onions, season with a little salt and cook while stirring until soft and glossy. Add the garlic, red bell pepper and bay leaf to the pan and cook, stirring, for 2–3 minutes. Squeeze in the tomato paste and gently mix. Pour in the wine and let the alcohol infuse the vegetables for 1 minute, then add the grated (shredded) tomatoes. Reduce the heat to medium-low, add the cinnamon stick, sweet paprika, allspice berries, orange zest, thyme sprigs and red chilli. Pour in 100ml (3½fl oz) of the warm vegetable broth or water. Simmer gently for about 20 minutes or until the sauce thickens. Remove and discard the bay leaf, cinnamon stick, thyme sprigs and dried or fresh chilli. Taste and adjust seasoning, if necessary, then mix in the parsley.

Lightly grease a large ovenproof dish with 2 tablespoons of the olive oil. Cover the base of the dish with the boiled chickpeas and spoon over one-third of the sauce, then stir to mix. Nestle the aubergines nicely between the chickpeas. Spoon the remaining sauce on top followed by the remaining broth and olive oil. Gently shake the baking dish to level.

Bake at 200°C/180°C fan/400°F/gas 6 for 30–40 minutes, uncovered, or until the aubergines are very soft and light brown and the sauce in the pan has reduced by half. Remove from the oven and let the dish stand for 10–15 minutes before serving.

Gemista **Stuffed tomatoes and peppers with potatoes**

FROM **AEGINA**

SERVES 4–6

- 300g (10½oz) Carolina or arborio rice (or any other medium-grained white rice)
- 6 large ripe tomatoes
- 6 green bell peppers
- 3 potatoes, peeled
- 1 teaspoon dried oregano
- 200ml (7fl oz) olive oil
- 1 large onion, peeled and finely chopped
- 1 bay leaf
- 2–3 garlic cloves, peeled and minced
- 1 carrot, peeled and grated (shredded)
- 1 courgette (zucchini), grated (shredded)
- 3 tablespoons chopped fresh parsley
- 3 tablespoons chopped fresh mint
- Sugar (optional)
- 3–4 teaspoons finely ground breadcrumbs
- Salt and freshly ground black pepper

This summer dish is cherished throughout Greece, including its islands. It often features a variety of seasonal vegetables hollowed and stuffed – or even courgette (zucchini) flowers and rolled leaves (such as grape leaves) – all combined in the same roasting tin (sheet pan) as seen on Crete. At times, the stuffing includes meat. Sometimes bulgur (cracked) wheat is used instead of rice, as commonly seen in the Dodecanese and especially on Rhodes. Here is the classic version of this dish to recreate at home and infuse your kitchen with delightful Mediterranean aromas.

This recipe holds a special place in my heart. It brings back memories of preparing the dish with my grandmother, Rena, in her summer kitchen on the island of Aegina. Despite having an oven, we took the prepared tray down the street to the local baker, who baked the entire neighbourhood's lunches in his wood-burning oven, each tray meticulously lined up with names. Just in time for lunch, we walked down the street again to retrieve it, savouring the wood-fired goodness on the stuffed veggies and potatoes. Here, I have opted for the convenience of a conventional oven, yielding consistently delightful results! Whether enjoyed warm, at room temperature or even straight from the fridge, this dish is a true delight, especially when served with feta and good bread. To elevate the experience even further, it pairs perfectly with a cold beer.

Rinse the rice under cold running water and then soak it in fresh cold water for 15 minutes. Drain the rice in a colander and set aside to dry.

Wash the tomatoes and bell peppers and pat them dry. Slice the tops of each tomato and pepper to create a lid. Using a teaspoon, carefully scoop out the flesh from the tomatoes without tearing the walls of the fruit. Place the tomato flesh in a food processor, blend it to make a tomato juice and set aside. Using a teaspoon, remove and discard the seeds and white membranes from the bell peppers. Lightly salt the insides of the tomatoes and peppers, then place them upside down in a large ovenproof dish, leaving space for the potatoes.

Cut the potatoes into rough 3cm (1 inch) chunks, place them in a bowl with ½ teaspoon of the dried oregano and season with salt and black pepper. Mix to coat and set aside.

Recipe continues overleaf

Heat a large, deep pan over a medium heat. Add 50ml (1¾fl oz) of the olive oil and, once hot, add the onion along with the bay leaf and sauté until soft. Add the garlic, grated carrot and courgette, then cook for 5 minutes or until they soften and most of their liquid evaporates. Add the rice and cook, stirring, for about 1 minute.

Set aside 250ml (9fl oz) of the blended tomato juice for later, then add the rest to the rice mixture, season with more salt and pepper to taste and cook for about 8 minutes until the rice has absorbed most of the liquid. Remove the pan from heat, remove and discard the bay leaf, and add the chopped fresh herbs. Mix well, then taste and adjust the seasoning, if necessary.

Preheat the oven to 190°C/170°C fan/375°F/gas 5.

Fill the tomatoes and bell peppers with the rice mixture, being careful not to overfill them as the rice will expand. Place them back in the ovenproof dish, leaving any leftover juices from the tomatoes in the dish, and cover with their lids. Arrange the potatoes around them in the dish.

In a blender, mix the reserved 250ml (9fl oz) tomato juice with 150ml (5fl oz) olive oil, 150ml (5fl oz) water, plus a little salt and pepper. Pour this blended tomato sauce over the stuffed tomatoes, bell peppers and potatoes in the dish and scatter over the breadcrumbs.

Place the dish on the bottom rack of the oven and bake for about 1 hour 10 minutes, or until everything is nicely browned. Remove the dish from the oven and let rest for at least 15 minutes before serving.

TIP

For a gluten-free version replace regular breadcrumbs with gluten-free breadcrumbs or omit completely.

THE ISLAND WINDMILLS

The iconic windmills are beloved symbols of the Greek islands. These charming structures were thoughtfully positioned to harness the wind's power most effectively while remaining accessible for islanders to transport wheat and flour using mules, donkeys, or even by hand. Nowadays, many old windmills have been preserved as tourist attractions or even private homes and hotels. The widespread presence of windmills across the islands highlights the vital role of grain production in these regions. In times when preserving food was crucial, the windmills played an essential role in grinding grains like wheat and barley, as well as other local seeds and pulses, such as fava (local yellow split peas, see page 40) on Santorini. When local production couldn't meet the demand, islands turned to others as they supplied each other with goods. Limnos has been particularly renowned for its flour since ancient times and was one of the main suppliers of flour for other Aegean islands. Until today, Limnos has quite a large and high-quality local flour production, including the native Aegean variety called Mavragani. Flour was primarily used to make bread, rusks, various types of pasta, and other staples in all island kitchens.

On most islands, bread was prepared on Saturdays to last through the week. Islanders would either bake it in their own ovens, if they had one, or take it to the local baker or a communal wood-burning oven, a tradition still upheld in some villages. Aside from the daily breads, there are festive bread recipes found across the Greek islands, some of which are very elaborate, like the wedding breads of Crete and the Easter breads of Rhodes. A stand-out among these special occasion breads is the eptazymo, made with a chickpea (garbanzo bean) starter and found on many islands such as Kalymnos, Zakynthos, Crete, Kos, Karpathos and Samothraki. This bread is quite challenging to make successfully, and there is a lot of superstition surrounding its preparation. It is said that the dough is very sensitive to 'the evil eye', so it should be prepared at night and in secret. The baker should be a woman, who must not speak a word while she kneads the dough. According to folklore from Zakynthos, fairies assist in the kneading process, and in other parts of Greece, they even dance during the crucial raising of the dough.

Rusks also played an important role in island life, offering a way to preserve bread for much longer. They are still very popular, and beyond the classic barley and wheat rusks, there are delightful traditional variations on every island, including the wonderful softer, wheat rusks with olive oil from Kythira, the carob rusks from Crete, and the saffron rusks from Astypalea. Each island boasts local pasta recipes, most of which are reminiscent of the many centuries of Venetian rule. Magiria and sioufihta from Crete, makarounes from Karpathos, aftoudia from Chios, flomaria from Limnos, and matsata from Folegandros, to name just a few. Aside from that, islanders make trahana, a granular wheat product made of flour, semolina, or coarsely cracked wheat. The most common types are dairy-based and are either boiled in milk – usually goats' milk or soured milk and/or yogurt. Small variations of trahana are found on different islands, such as xinohodro in Crete and hachles in Lesvos.

Some pasta dishes are very humble, peasant fare, where the pasta is cooked with milk like porridge, either savoury or even sweet, with sugar and cinnamon added. Examples include mas from Tinos, which resembles tagliatelle, or aranista from Naxos and the small Cyclades (also known as ardista in Astypalaia), which resemble small, trahanas-like pasta. Pasta is also added to soups like the lentil soup in Astypalea or the fish soups prepared on Lesvos and Limnos. On Greek islands, pasta is often paired with meat, fish, or seafood. Some beloved examples include pastitsada from Corfu, matsata with cockerel from Folegandros, mirmitzeli with octopus from Paros and Antiparos, and the popular astakomakaronada with lobster (see page 62) found on several islands, including Skyros. From festive breads to distinctive pasta dishes, the Greek islands offer a captivating culinary journey through cherished traditions that celebrate community and creativity.

Tsimetia **Stuffed courgette flowers and chard dolmades with rice and herbs**

GF

FROM **IOS**

SERVES 6

350–400g (12½–14oz) large chard leaves, trimmed from stem
12 courgette (zucchini) flowers
160ml (5fl oz) olive oil
2 tablespoons fresh lemon juice
300ml (10fl oz) lukewarm water
Salt and freshly ground black pepper
Strained Greek-style yogurt, to serve

FOR THE FILLING

250g (9oz) Carolina or arborio rice
1 very large ripe tomato (about 300g/10oz)
2 medium onions, finely chopped (about 220g/8oz)
5 spring onions (scallions), finely chopped
1 carrot, grated (shredded)
5–6 tablespoons chopped fresh mint (reserve the stems)
4 tablespoons chopped fresh parsley (reserve the stems)
3 tablespoons chopped fresh dill
1 tablespoon fresh lemon juice
1½ teaspoons salt
1 teaspoon freshly ground black pepper
2 tablespoons olive oil

Courgette (zucchini) flowers are celebrated across the Greek islands and are used in various delectable ways, although most often stuffed. Whether filled with cheese and fried or stuffed with bulgur (cracked) wheat or rice and baked in a pot, both methods have their allure and never fail to delight. Known as *tsimetia* on Ios and enhanced with chopped wild fennel fronds on Astypalea, each rendition has its own unique flair. On Crete, a touch of ground cumin infuses the flowers with extra spice.

It's not uncommon to find a medley of dolmades in the same pot as the stuffed courgette flowers, something I often do for variety and practicality. In this recipe, chard dolmades and courgette flowers utilise the same filling mixture. Alternatively, vine leaves or other large green leaves, like sorrel or collard greens, can be used for the dolmades. If courgette flowers are unavailable, simply substitute with your preferred leaves, adjusting the blanching time as needed based on their thickness. To make this dish, it's essential to use a wide, shallow, heavy-based pot to ensure even cooking without squashing the ingredients by stacking them in too many layers. These will store well in the fridge for a couple of days, so pray for leftovers!

First, prepare the chard leaves. Fill a large pan with water and bring it to the boil over a medium-high heat. Remove the pan from the heat and blanch the chard leaves, a few at a time, for about 20 seconds until they soften and become flexible enough to bend and roll. Transfer the leaves to a bowl of iced water to cool, then drain and let dry in a colander for about 20 minutes.

Meanwhile, gently remove the stamens from inside the courgette flowers, then trim any outer green leaves and stems at the base. Carefully rinse the flowers, ensuring not to tear the petals, and shake off any excess water. Arrange the flowers on paper towels and leave to dry.

Next, make the filling. Rinse the rice under cold running water, drain well in a colander, then place it in a large mixing bowl. Using the large holes of a box grater, grate the tomato into the bowl, discarding the skin. Stir in the chopped onions, spring onions, grated carrot, chopped herbs and lemon juice. Season well with the salt and freshly ground black pepper. Finally, stir in the 2 tablespoons of olive oil and mix well.

Arrange the reserved mint and parsley stems over the base of a wide, shallow, heavy-based pot with a lid. Set aside the largest, intact chard leaves for rolling the dolmades. Lay any small or torn leaves over the herbs in a single layer in the pot.

To stuff the courgette flowers, place 1–1½ heaped teaspoons of filling into each flower (depending on their size), then fold the petals over to enclose it.

To roll the dolmades, place a chard leaf in front of you with the veins right side up. If the stem is thick, trim the stem by cutting it out in an upside-down V shape. This ensures that the leaves are easier to roll and will cook evenly. Place about 1–1½ heaped teaspoons of the filling in the lower centre of the leaf (depending on the leaf's size) and fold the left side of the leaf over the filling, then the right side, and roll up from the bottom to the top to make a neat roll.

Lay the stuffed courgette flowers and rolled chard leaves closely together in the pot, arranging them in a spiral pattern with the seam sides down to prevent them from opening while cooking. Season each layer with salt and pepper. For the next layer, repeat the spiral arrangement.

Once all the filled flowers and leaves are arranged in the pot, pour in the olive oil and lemon juice. Turn a plate upside down and place it on top of the stuffed flowers and leaves in the centre of the pot to keep them from opening and preserve their shape. Pour in the lukewarm water and cover the pot with a lid. Bring to a boil over a medium-high heat, then reduce the heat to medium-low and simmer for 20 minutes. Lower the heat again and gently simmer for a further 20 minutes. (The total cooking time is just over 40 minutes.)

Remove the pot from the heat, take off the lid and let everything cool slightly before carefully lifting off the plate using a thick dish towel or oven mitt. Let the stuffed courgette flowers and dolmades stand for 20–30 minutes before serving at room temperature, or even cold from the fridge. Enjoy with a spoonful of yogurt on the side.

Gamopilafo **Wedding pilaf**

FROM **CRETE**

SERVES 4–6

FOR THE STOCK
- 2kg (4lb 8oz) free-range or organic whole chicken
- 2 chicken thighs (optional)
- Salt

FOR THE RICE
- 400g (14oz) Carolina, arborio or Valencia rice
- 1.2 litres (40fl oz) homemade chicken stock (see above)
- 2 tablespoons olive oil
- 4–5 tablespoons fresh lemon juice
- 3 tablespoons *staka* (or use good-quality ewes' milk butter or cows' milk butter)
- Salt and freshly ground black pepper

Gamopilafo, which translates as 'wedding pilaf', is a festive dish prepared in large quantities at Cretan weddings and other significant celebrations. Symbolising abundance and good luck, rice is perfectly suited for such occasions. This dish embodies Cretan cuisine, characterised by its simplicity and mastery of flavour through minimal yet excellent ingredients. The key here is the homemade chicken stock, which must be rich and flavourful. Traditionally, Cretans use generous amounts of meat, typically yearly lamb or goat and chicken, to create a deep stock. For a lighter version prepared at home, chicken alone is used. The finishing touch is melted *staka*, a traditional Cretan dairy product akin to clarified butter or ghee in its consistency, which is poured hot over the rice to create a creamy texture and unique flavour.

This recipe has been handed down through generations of the Mamidaki family from Anoskeli village, where they produce exceptional olive oil and wine. Holding a special place in the family's culinary heritage, it was passed down to my friend Eleftheria Mamidaki from her aunts Rita, Erasmia, and Katina. It was initially created by Eleftheria's grandmother, Irene, during a time when goat or lamb meat was scarce, so instead she used chickens from her coop to make the stock, resulting in a lighter, healthier version. The dish always incorporates the family's exceptional olive oil and is frequently paired with Romeiko wine, a sweet white grape variety indigenous to the region, bottled by their own winery located in the same village.

Place the whole chicken and chicken thighs, if using, in a large pot with a lid. Pour in enough water to cover the chicken and add a pinch of salt. Bring it to a gentle simmer over a medium heat, skimming off any foam that rises to the surface. Cover the pot with the lid, leaving it slightly ajar, and let the chicken simmer over low heat for about 1 hour 30 minutes. If necessary, top up the pot with boiling water to keep the chicken submerged. (If the heat is kept low, additional water may not be needed.) To check if the chicken is thoroughly cooked, pierce it with a fork; the meat should be tender and fall off the bones. The chicken should be slightly overcooked so the flavours and fat are released into the broth. Remove the pot from the heat and strain the contents through a fine sieve (strainer). The broth should be slightly oily and rich in flavour. Adjust the seasoning with salt – the broth should be well-seasoned. Set aside the poached chicken.

Meanwhile, rinse the rice thoroughly under cold running water. Cover the rice with lukewarm water and leave to soak in for 20 minutes. Drain in a colander and set aside.

Recipe continues overleaf

Measure out the 1.2 litres (40fl oz) stock needed to cook 400g (14oz) rice. (If you are cooking a substantial amount of rice for a feast, the amount stock needed is based on the number of portions. The rice-to-stock ratio is one part rice to three parts stock. This means that for every 100g (3½oz) rice, you will need 300ml (10fl oz) stock.) Remember to set aside 200ml (7fl oz) stock for the finishing touch.

Place a wide, shallow pan over a medium-high heat. Add the olive oil and, once hot, tip the rice into the pan, stirring a few times to coat the grains with the oil. Next, add the measured stock and gently stir. When it starts to simmer, lower the heat and continue to cook while stirring gently. Season with salt to taste and simmer for 10 minutes, then stir in 2–3 tablespoons lemon juice to taste. Do not to overcook the rice – it should be al dente, like a risotto. Once the rice is tender, remove the pan from the heat, cover it with a clean dish towel and let the rice sit for 10 minutes to absorb the liquid.

Meanwhile, melt 50g (1¾oz) of the staka or butter in a small pan over a low heat, then heat it until sizzling. Uncover the rice and pour over the hot staka or butter, stir gently and then cover the pan again with the towel and leave for a further 5–10 minutes.

Preheat the oven to 180°C/160°C fan/350°F/gas 4.

While you wait for the rice, prepare the chicken. Divide about 1kg (2lb 4oz) of the poached chicken meat into small portions, either removing the bones and skin and plating only the meat or leaving it intact and dividing into portions. (Any remaining chicken can be stored for later or used in another recipe, such as a soup using the leftover stock.) Arrange the chicken portions in an ovenproof dish, then season with the remaining lemon juice, salt and freshly ground black pepper. Pour about 200ml (7fl oz) of the reserved stock over the chicken.

Place the dish in the hot oven and bake for 15 minutes, or until the chicken pieces are warmed through and lightly golden. Once ready, serve the chicken alongside large spoonfuls of the rice.

NOTE

For the traditional lamb-infused version, add a small leg of lamb to the stock instead of the chicken thighs. Keep in mind that unless you are cooking for a large gathering, this recipe will yield more stock than needed for this recipe. Any leftover stock can be stored in the fridge or freezer and used in other recipes. A simple stock like this is always a valuable and versatile kitchen staple.

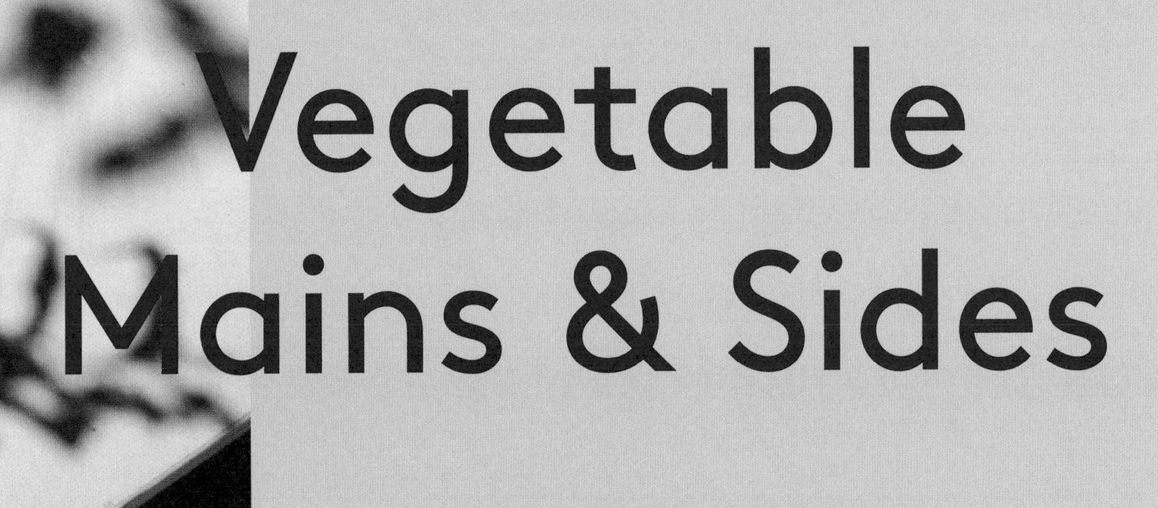

Vegetable Mains & Sides

CHAPTER 7

Bamies sto fourno **Baked okra with feta and mint**

FROM **LEROS**

SERVES 4–6

1kg (2lb 4oz) small okra, fresh or frozen, trimmed
1 tablespoon sea salt (if using fresh okra)
4 tablespoons vinegar (if using fresh okra)
800g (1lb 12oz) cherry tomatoes
200ml (7fl oz) olive oil
2 red onions, halved and thinly sliced
3–4 garlic cloves, peeled and roughly chopped
2 bay leaves
1½ teaspoons dried marjoram
40ml (3 tablespoons) red wine vinegar
100g (3½oz) feta
2 tablespoons chopped parsley
3 tablespoons chopped mint
Salt and freshly ground black pepper

During the summer months, okra thrives across the islands and holds a special place on traditional taverna menus. Typically smaller and less seeded than its larger counterpart, Greek okra is a staple in island kitchens where it's often prepared as a hearty stew in a fresh tomato sauce with onions and garlic. This flavourful dish frequently accompanies chicken or beef, stewed or baked together, or finds itself alongside fish, such as a whole grouper or parrot fish, as they do on Crete.

On Leros, okra is usually baked and is a summer classic. I personally prefer baked to stewed okra due to its texture and I'm proud to say that I've converted many people who thought they hated okra into okra lovers! I also like to enhance them with a generous splash of vinegar. I find the acidity complements both the okra's robust flavours and the creamy richness of feta, plus it keeps the okra firm. For a vegan version, you can omit the feta without sacrificing the dish's essence. Fresh herbs and tomatoes are essential here in my opinion; I opt for cherry tomatoes due to their natural sweetness, reminiscent of the luscious, vibrant flavour of Greek island tomatoes that make everything taste delicious.

If using fresh okra, wash them under cold running water, then trim and pat dry. Arrange the okra in a single layer on a tray, sprinkle with sea salt and vinegar, then gently toss to coat. Let them dry for 1–2 hours, ideally in the sun. Thoroughly rinse the okra and drain well. To prevent them turning slimy, ensure the okra are completely dry before cooking.

If using frozen okra, cook them directly from the freezer but first remove any ice that is attached and dry them a paper towel. Cooking directly from frozen helps the okra keep their shape.

Place half the cherry tomatoes in a blender and blitz until smooth. Quarter the remaining tomatoes and set aside.

In a large, deep pan, heat 4 tablespoons of the olive oil over medium heat. Add the okra and sauté for 4–5 minutes, tossing gently. Add the quartered tomatoes, onions, garlic, bay leaves and marjoram to the pan. Season with sea salt and freshly ground black pepper and cook, stirring, for a further 2 minutes.

Pour the red wine vinegar into the pan with the okra and let it evaporate for 1 minute before adding the blitzed cherry tomatoes. Lower the heat and gently simmer for 2 minutes. Remove the pan from heat and adjust the seasoning if needed, but make allowances for the salty feta that will be added later.

Preheat your oven to 200°C/180°C fan/400°F/gas 6.

Transfer the contents of the pan to a large, deep ovenproof dish; if possible, arrange everything in a single layer. Drizzle with the remaining olive oil, then gently toss. Cover the dish with parchment paper and foil, or a well-fitting lid.

Bake the okra in the hot oven, covered, for 30 minutes. Uncover the dish, crumble over the feta, then scatter on the chopped parsley and mint and toss to mix. Bake for a further 20–30 minutes uncovered, mixing everything together halfway through the cooking time. The okra should look slightly charred and caramelised, while the sauce has reduced and thickened. Remove the dish from the oven and let it stand, uncovered, for 10–15 minutes before serving. This allows the flavours to mingle, so the longer you let it stand the better it tastes.

Serve the okra with a good grinding of black pepper. Some crusty bread alongside soaks up the flavourful sauce.

BAKED OKRA OMELETTE

Across the islands, it's customary to repurpose any leftovers into hearty omelettes. Likewise, the leftovers from this recipe transform wonderfully into a second meal with eggs. Feel free to experiment with various leftovers for more delicious results!

Spoon about 5–6 tablespoons of leftover okra (either straight from the fridge or at room temperature) into a large pan and place over a medium heat. Beat 4–5 eggs in a bowl with a little salt and black pepper. Pour the beaten egg on top of the okra and let it cook for 3–4 minutes. Carefully flip the omelette onto the other side to cook evenly.

Patates tiganites **The ultimate fried potatoes**

FROM **NAXOS**

I don't know anyone who doesn't have a soft spot for fried potatoes. I'm talking about fresh, hand-cut potatoes – whether thinly sliced, thickly cut or shaped like round chips – perfectly fried in olive oil so they are soft on the inside, yet delightfully crispy and golden on the outside. Any Greek taverna known for its excellent fresh, hand-cut fried potatoes is always a hit. They are not just a side but often feature as a starter, shared with tzatziki, salad and other nibbles. When they're good, there is never enough! Around the islands you will find fried potatoes siding several dishes, mostly grilled meats and saucy stews, with rich tomato or fragrant lemon sauces. They are also commonly served with fried meatballs or eggs, with feta and good bread on the side.

The best fried potatoes I've ever eaten were on the Greek islands. Locally grown, especially in the Cyclades, they turn quite yellow when fried. When served on their own, fried potatoes are not only seasoned with sea salt but also sprinkled with dried oregano – a very popular combination. Some people like to drizzle them with lemon juice or sprinkle them with paprika, feta or hard grated (shredded) cheeses such as *kefalotyri* (similar to pecorino). Here I am suggesting a classic serve with crumbled feta and oregano. For a vegan option omit the feta but keep the oregano.

Making perfect fried potatoes at home is a breeze. There are various techniques for achieving good results, but I find the double-frying method is the most foolproof approach. Let's go through some general rules that are always good to know.

POTATOES

Not all potatoes are suitable for frying. Generally, those with a yellowish hue and a good balance of starch and moisture are considered the best. The top varieties for frying are: Maris Piper, King Edward, Russet, Yukon Gold and, in Greece, the Naxos island potatoes. Freshness is equally important. Sprouting potatoes convert starch into sugar, which isn't conducive to frying. Fresh potatoes will feel firm, be free of sprouts or green spots and without wrinkly skin. It's also important that the potatoes are cut to a uniform size for even frying.

SALT

Choose a good sea salt. I love to use fleur de sel on fried potatoes, which I always keep in stock at home.

Recipe continues overleaf

SOAKING AND DRYING

As soon as you peel or cut the potatoes, place them in a large bowl of fresh water. This prevents them from browning and helps to remove any excess starch, for a crispier result. After soaking for at least 30 minutes (you can even soak them overnight), drain and thoroughly dry them with paper towels, making sure they are as dry as possible when they go into the hot oil.

FRYING

The following instructions are for potatoes cut into sticks about 1cm (⅓ inch) thick. Depending on their size, you may need to adjust the cooking times slightly. Use a large, deep frying pan (skillet) or heavy-based pot that can accommodate plenty of oil without the risk of splattering. Place the pan over a medium heat. Pour in enough olive oil to fill about one-third of the pan, ensuring that the oil is at least 3cm (1 inch) deep. Heat the oil to 150°C/300°F. If you do not have a kitchen thermometer, you can check the temperature by dropping in a potato stick. (It is a misconception that you can't fry in olive oil. When the quality is good, you can perfectly fry in it up to 200°C/400°F.)

FIRST FRYING (BLANCHING)

Work in batches to prevent a sudden drop in oil temperature and ensure the potatoes blanch evenly. Carefully lower the potato sticks, a handful at a time, into the hot oil and cook at 150°C/300°F to 165°C/330°F for about 5 minutes. They should look pale and feel soft but not yet be fully cooked or golden and crisp. Using a slotted spoon, lift the potato sticks out of the pan onto a tray and let them cool for 10 minutes. Be gentle with them at this stage as they are soft, tender and may break.

SECOND FRYING

Increase the heat to raise the temperature of the oil to 180°C/350°F. Working in batches, fry the potato sticks again for about 3 minutes or until they turn golden and crispy. As soon as they are golden and crispy, remove them with a slotted spoon and drain on a tray line with paper towels.

SEASONING

Sprinkle some salt onto the fried potato sticks (but don't overdo the salt if you are adding feta) and gently toss them. Transfer the potatoes to a plate, crumble some feta (or other cheese) over the top (if using), then add a pinch of dried oregano.

Enjoy the fried potatoes immediately!

Delagratsiano **Layered aubergine and potato bake**

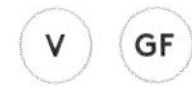

FROM **SYROS**

SERVES 6

FOR THE VEGETABLES

1kg (2lb 4oz) aubergines (eggplants), cut lengthwise into 1cm (⅓ inch) slices
1kg (2lb 4oz) potatoes, peeled and cut lengthwise into 1cm (⅓ inch) slices
Olive oil, for frying or roasting
Salt and freshly ground black pepper

FOR THE TOMATO SAUCE

1kg (2lb 4oz) ripe tomatoes or cherry tomatoes
60ml (2fl oz) olive oil
1 onion, chopped
3 garlic cloves, peeled and roughly chopped
1 heaped teaspoon tomato paste (concentrated puree)
1 bay leaf
50ml (1¾fl oz) sweet red wine, such as Mavrodaphne
1 fresh thyme sprig
1 small cinnamon stick
Pinch of ground cloves
2 tablespoons chopped parsley
Salt and freshly ground black pepper

FOR THE BECHAMEL

1 litre (34fl oz) milk
100ml (3½fl oz) olive oil
100g (3½oz) plain (all-purpose) flour
100g (3½oz) feta, crumbled
¼ teaspoon ground nutmeg
Salt and freshly ground black pepper

This dish takes its name from Delagratsia, one of the most picturesque and affluent areas on the island of Syros, the capital of the Cyclades. Nowadays called Posidonia (its original ancient name), Delagratsia is situated on the south-western coast of the island. During the Venetian rule, the area was named Della Grazia after the small Catholic church of Madonna della Gratsia, which still stands north of the settlement. The area is celebrated for its elegant nineteenth-century neoclassical mansions, breathtaking beaches and lush gardens, which all showcase the island's rich history and cultural heritage.

The recipe is inspired by a peasant dish made with aubergines, potatoes, tomatoes and cheese. The traditional version is simpler and does not include bechamel, but some later variations do. My version is more like a vegetarian moussaka; I find that the bechamel binds everything together nicely and makes it a more satisfying meal. I love mixing in some feta, which adds flavour. The vegetables can be grilled, pan-fried or even air-fried. You can also add more vegetables to the layers, such as red bell peppers or courgettes (zucchini).

Soak the aubergine slices in salted lukewarm water for 15–30 minutes, while you prepare the sauce.

Meanwhile, make the sauce. If using larger ripe tomatoes, grate them using the large holes of a box grater, discarding the skins. If using cherry tomatoes, put them in a blender and blitz until smooth.

Place a large, deep pan over a medium-high heat. Add 3 tablespoons of the olive oil, then added the onion and sauté with a pinch of salt. Once soft, add in the garlic, tomato paste and bay leaf, then stir to mix everything together.

Pour in the wine and let the alcohol evaporate for 1 minute. Add in the tomatoes, thyme, cinnamon stick and ground cloves. Lower the heat and season with salt and pepper. Cover the pan, leaving the lid slightly ajar, and simmer until the sauce thickens, about 25 minutes depending on how juicy the tomatoes are. Remove and discard the bay leaf, cinnamon stick, and thyme, then mix in the remaining olive oil and the chopped parsley. Adjust the seasoning, if necessary. Continue to gently simmer over a very low heat for a further 5 minutes, then set aside.

Drain the aubergine and pat dry with paper towels. Pat the potatoes dry too.

Recipe continues overleaf

If frying the vegetables, place a frying pan (skillet) over a medium-high heat and pour in enough olive oil to cover the base. Working in batches, fry the aubergines and potatoes, turning them frequently, until golden on all sides – they don't need to be cooked all the way through. Place the cooked aubergines and potatoes on a tray lined with paper towels to absorb any excess oil. Season with salt and pepper.

If roasting the vegetables, preheat oven to 190°C/170°C fan/375°F/gas 5. Line three large baking trays with parchment paper. Arrange the aubergines and potatoes on the trays in a single layer, ideally separating each type on different trays. Brush them with olive oil and season with salt and pepper. Place the potatoes on the top racks of the oven and the aubergines on the bottom racks and roast for 15 minutes or until the vegetables are tender and golden. Turn them over and roast for a further 5–10 minutes or until golden, switching racks if necessary. Remove the trays from the oven and season the vegetables with salt and pepper.

Meanwhile, make the bechamel sauce. Heat the milk in a large saucepan over a medium heat. Place another large saucepan over a medium heat and add the olive oil. Once warm, add the flour and whisk continuously to form a pale paste (roux). Whisking continuously, gradually add the warm milk to the paste until the mixture thickens to a medium consistency. Once ready, remove the pan from heat, stir in the feta and season with the ground nutmeg, salt and pepper to taste.

Preheat the oven to 180°C/160°C fan/350°F/gas 4.

To assemble the bake, cover the base of a large, deep baking dish (I use one that is 30 x 23 x 7cm/12 x 9 x 3 inches) with about 3 tablespoons of the tomato sauce. Scatter over 2 tablespoons of the grated (shredded) cheese and add a layer of the potatoes. Spoon 2 tablespoons of the tomato sauce over the potatoes, sprinkle with 2 tablespoons of the grated cheese, then add a layer of the aubergines on top. Spoon over 3–4 tablespoons of the tomato sauce and then crumble over the feta. Season with pepper. Drizzle over 4–5 tablespoons of the bechamel sauce. Repeat these layers once more with the remaining potatoes and aubergines. Pour the remaining tomato sauce over the final layer of aubergines, then spread the last of the bechamel sauce evenly over the top. Sprinkle with the remaining grated cheese.

Bake in the hot oven for 50 minutes or until a golden crust has formed on top of the bake. When ready, remove the dish from the oven and let cool for 20 minutes before serving.

FORAGED GREENS AND HERBS

The Greek islands boast an extraordinary biodiversity, fostered by their isolation, diverse landscapes and climatic variations. Within this, numerous endemic edible plant species thrive, forming the cornerstone of local cuisines and medicinal practices. These botanical treasures are celebrated for their abundance of vital nutrients and antioxidants, contributing significantly to the renowned health benefits associated with the Mediterranean diet.

For islanders, foraging is not just a means of sustenance but an integral part of their cultural heritage. They possess an intimate knowledge of the land, skilfully gathering a bounty of wild treasures that dot their surroundings. For islanders, foraging is a way to gather food, but it's a deeply ingrained cultural practice that connects them to their surroundings. They have a deep understanding of the land and its resources, harvesting everything from capers and samphire to borage, figs, almonds and even saffron. Incorporating these wild gifts into their culinary traditions, islanders infuse their dishes with a depth of flavour and nutritional richness that speaks to the land's bounty. Moreover, these indigenous plants offer not only sustenance but also serve as remedies in traditional medicine, providing relief to those who partake.

Indeed, the foraged delights of the Greek islands stand as a testament to the enduring connection between people and nature, weaving a tapestry of flavours and healing that enriches both body and soul. These wild ingredients infuse their dishes with a richness and nutritional goodness that reflects the natural abundance of the islands. In addition to their culinary uses, many of these plants have medicinal properties and are used in traditional remedies passed down through generations. This close relationship between people and nature is a defining aspect of island life, shaping both the cuisine and the culture of the Greek islands.

Edible wild greens, or horta as they are commonly called in Greece, vary seasonally. These greens are often enjoyed as salads, either boiled or raw where appropriate, and drizzled with olive oil and fresh lemon juice or sometimes vinegar. They are also added to omelettes, stews and pies, stir-fried (known as tsigariasta or tsigarelia), or cooked with rice, other grains or pulses. Some of these greens are bitter, others are milder or even slightly sweet and very aromatic. The textures also vary, with some greens being rougher and others tender and velvety. My favourite greens are those mixed while foraged, even more so when they have a few herbs mixed in, offering a variety of flavours and textures, and providing valuable nutrients and antioxidants. When drizzled with a good olive oil and some lemon juice they become a true superfood.

On the island of Crete, greens are often boiled along with a whole onion and tomato, which adds flavour and sweetness. The boiled tomato is mushed and used as a topping for the greens.

On many islands, they simply dress the greens with a grated fresh tomato and a drizzle of olive oil. Most restaurant menus around Greece will simply call it horta and will serve what is in season. Some common greens that you would come across during summer at restaurants around the Greek islands include vlita (Amaranth greens), which are mild and tender, and antrakla (purslane), which is pleasantly sour and crunchy and great in salads but can also be cooked. Another common green that often accompanies seafood is monk's beard (saltwort), known in Greece as almyra. It has a delightful salty flavour as it grows near the sea, and its texture resembles seaweed when boiled.

Wild herbs are highly esteemed. They are used fresh and are also dried to preserve. Apart from cooking and baking, herbs feature in cheeses, liqueurs and distilled drinks, savoury and sweet dishes, breads, rusks and cookies. It's common to see abundant bunches of oregano and thymbra hanging upside down in courtyards and kitchens. In those kitchens, you'll find dozens of jars brimming with a wonderful array of dried herbs, stored for year-round cooking.

Thymbra capitata, colloquially known as throubi, resembles thyme but boasts a spicier, more robust flavour, making it a prevalent herb across many islands. Fennel, thyme, lavender, oregano, chamomile, bay leaves, rosemary, sage and marjoram are some of the common herbs found on many islands. On the Ionian Islands, marjoram is particularly popular and is referred to as sapsycho. Additionally, unique herbs like the delightful fliskouni (Teucrium polium), sometimes termed 'felty germander' in English, as well as the Cretan Dittany (Origanum dictamnus) and Mountain Tea (Sideritis syriaca), add to the herbal diversity. These herbs are prominently featured in teas and are integral to traditional medicinal practices passed down through generations.

Soufiko **Braised summer vegetables**

FROM **IKARIA**

SERVES 4

- 1 aubergine (eggplant, about 370g/13oz)
- 2 onions
- 2 potatoes (about 280g/10oz)
- 1 large courgette (zucchini, about 180g/6oz)
- 2 large ripe tomatoes (about 640g/1lb 6oz), peeled
- 200ml (7fl oz) olive oil
- 3 garlic cloves, peeled and thinly sliced
- 1 bay leaf
- 2 Romano peppers, deseeded
- 1–2 hot green chillies (depending on their size and how spicy you like it), deseeded
- 350g green beans, trimmed and halved
- 160ml (5½fl oz) red wine
- 1–2 small basil sprigs or 4–5 whole leaves
- Salt and freshly ground black pepper

This delightful dish hails from Ikaria, a 'blue zone' island celebrated for its breathtaking landscapes, the vibrant outdoor festivals (*panigyria*) and the relaxed lifestyle of its locals. Their diet is primarily plant based, rich in vegetables, fruits, legumes, olive oil, locally produced honeys and only moderate amounts of fish, meat and dairy. Legend has it that *soufiko* was created by accident when a woman, having forgotten to prepare her husband's dinner, hurriedly picked whatever vegetables were available in her garden and tossed them into a pan. The result was so delicious that, after tasting it, she began muttering in the local dialect, '*sou fiko, den sou fiko!*' (I will leave you some, I won't leave you any!)

It's important to use the freshest vegetables, which are firm and juicy as they are stewed in their own liquids rather than any water being added during the cooking process. And be generous with the olive oil in this recipe – it really makes a difference. It's why this dish is so heavenly delicious, but it tastes even better the next day! I like to add basil, but you can also try parsley. Greeks typically serve this dish with a cheese, such as feta, and a rustic crusty bread.

Using a peeler, partially peel the aubergine to create stripes, then cut it into rough 2.5cm (1 inch) chunks. Soak the aubergine chunks in salted lukewarm water for 15–20 minutes while you prepare the rest of the vegetables.

Cut the remaining vegetables, including the tomatoes, into similar-sized 2.5cm (1 inch) pieces, reserving any juices.

Drain the aubergine and pat dry with paper towels.

Place a wide, shallow pan with a well-fitting lid over a medium-high heat. Pour in half the olive oil, then add the onions, potatoes, garlic and bay leaf and cooking, stirring, until the onions soften. Add the aubergines, peppers and chillies, then stir for a couple of minutes before adding the courgette and green beans. Stir to coat all the vegetables in olive oil and season with salt and pepper.

Pour in the wine and let the alcohol cook off for a couple of minutes, while gently tossing the vegetables. Add the tomatoes to the pan, along with their juices, and the basil. Season with salt and pepper to taste. Turn down the heat to medium-low and cover the pan with the lid, leaving it slightly ajar. Cook for 30 minutes or until the vegetables are almost done. Remove the lid and cook for a further 10–15 minutes uncovered, until most of the liquid has evaporated. Remove and discard the bay leaf, then taste and adjust the seasoning, if necessary. Reduce the heat to low and add the remaining olive oil, then let it cook over a very low heat for a further 15 minutes. Remove the pan from heat and let it stand for at least 20 minutes before serving.

Aginaropita **Cheesy artichoke gratin**

FROM **TINOS**

SERVES 6

6 trimmed artichokes, fresh or frozen
80ml (2½fl oz) olive oil
1 large leek, chopped (green part too, if tender)
1 onion, chopped
3 spring onions (scallions), chopped (green parts too, if fresh)
2 carrots, diced
2 courgettes (zucchini), diced
4–5 tablespoons chopped parsley
4–5 tablespoons chopped dill
Salt and freshly ground black pepper

FOR THE SAUCE
4 eggs
100ml (3½fl oz) crème fraiche
200ml (7fl oz) whole (full-fat) milk
150g (5½oz) Parmesan, grated (shredded)
160g (6oz) *anthotiro* or ricotta
150g (5½oz) feta, well crumbled or grated (shredded) in the large hole of a box grater

Tinos holds a special place in my heart and so does its cuisine. This beautiful island, renowned for its mineral-rich soil, yields exceptional wines and the most flavourful artichokes. Apart from the distinctive purple cultivated variety, fields of wild artichokes thrive – they have a much shorter season, are smaller in size and have fewer, thicker leaves and formidable thorns. Despite the challenging trimming process, these wild artichokes are incredibly rewarding in flavour and cherished by locals. They are usually preserved in olive oil or vinegar, serving as a traditional meze paired perfectly with the local *raki*, a grape distillate infused with fennel.

Every restaurant on Tinos proudly features artichokes on their menu, showcasing their versatility in dishes ranging from fried and stewed to stuffed or baked. One stand-out local recipe is *aginaropita*, an artichoke pie that is usually made without pastry and leans more towards a soufflé or a gratin, enriched with vegetables, eggs and cheeses. Traditional versions often incorporate thin slices of stale bread, lending a delightful bread pudding-like texture. One of my favourite versions of this dish comes from Eleni's colourful taverna called To Koutouki tis Elenis, which is nestled in the narrow alleys of Tinos town. Eleni's taverna has been a beloved spot on the island for decades, renowned for serving authentic local recipes and homemade cheeses. Inspired by Eleni's culinary prowess, I've adapted her recipe a bit by using frozen artichokes and substituting local cheeses with more readily available options that deliver a similarly delicious result.

Chop the artichokes into rough 1.5cm (½ inch) pieces. Brush a deep baking dish (I use one 30 x 23cm/12 x 9 inches) with olive oil.

Place a large, deep pan over a medium-high heat. Add the olive oil, then add the leek, onion and spring onions and sauté until soft. Add the carrots and courgettes, then season with a little salt and pepper and cook, stirring occasionally, for 10 minutes or until softened. There should be no liquid left in the pan; if there is, drain off any excess liquid or cook for a bit longer until it evaporates. Transfer the vegetables to the oiled baking dish, spreading them out evenly with the back of a spoon or a spatula.

Preheat the oven to 180°C/160°C fan/360°F/gas 4.

In a separate bowl, beat the eggs until frothy and then mix in the crème fraiche and milk. Set aside half of the Parmesan for the topping, then stir all three cheeses into the sauce. Pour the cheese sauce over the vegetables and scatter over the remaining Parmesan.

Bake the gratin in the hot oven for 50–60 minutes or until the sauce is bubbling and the top is golden.

Sympetherio **Summer vegetable roast**

VE GF

FROM **CRETE**

SERVES 4–6

- 1 aubergine (eggplant, about 380g/13oz)
- 450g (1lb) potatoes, peeled
- 2 carrots (about 250g/9oz), peeled
- 1 large or 2 small courgettes (zucchini, about 200g/7oz)
- 2 onions (about 260g/9½oz)
- 1 leek
- 2 Romano peppers (about 140g/5oz)
- 1 or 2 spicy peppers (optional)
- 2 sweet green peppers (about 140g/4oz)
- 2 ripe tomatoes (500g/1lb 2oz)
- 30g (8½oz) sweet baby plum or cherry tomatoes, halved
- 3–4 small garlic cloves, peeled but left whole
- Bunch of parsley, roughly chopped
- 1 heaped teaspoon ground cumin
- 100ml (3½fl oz) dry white wine
- 100ml (3½fl oz) olive oil
- Sea salt and freshly ground black pepper

Sympetherio is a seasonal mix of garden vegetables. I love the Greek name they use in western Crete for this popular summer dish: *sympetherio* refers to the bond that forms between the two families of spouses. While you can't pick your in-laws, you must learn to live in harmony with them – just like vegetables tossed together in the same pan!

There's no strict rule about which vegetables to use – anything in season works. In winter, you can replace the aubergine (eggplant) and courgettes (zucchini) with cabbage, broccoli or cauliflower. It's a fantastic way to use up any vegetables and for a very healthy meal. The key is to use fresh vegetables so their juices are released during cooking, avoiding the need to add water and making the dish more flavourful. This dish is usually cooked on the stove top, but I prefer to cook it in the oven, just as everyone in my family always has. The vegetables keep their shape better, turning deliciously soft inside and slightly crusty outside. I also add cumin, a spice cherished on Crete, which makes our house smell like summer. This dish is one of my favourites because it's easy to make. I pair it with feta, bread and a cold beer!

Trim the stem from the aubergine, cut it lengthwise into quarters and then into 2cm (⅔ inch) slices. Soak the aubergine slices in lukewarm salted water for 30 minutes, then pat dry with paper towels. Meanwhile, prepare the other vegetables. Slice the potatoes, carrots and courgettes into 2cm (⅔ inch) rounds. Quarter the onions and cut each quarter in half. Cut the leek lengthwise and then into 2cm (⅔ inch) slices. Slice the peppers into 2cm (⅔ inch) thick pieces.

Preheat the oven to 190°C/170°C/375°F/gas 5.

Pick a deep roasting tin (sheet pan) that will fit all the vegetables in a single layer. Using the large holes of a box grater, grate (shred) the tomatoes directly into the tin. Discard the skins. Add all the prepared vegetables to the tin, along with the halved baby or cherry tomatoes, garlic and parsley. Sprinkle over the cumin and season generously with salt and pepper.

In a jug (pitcher), combine the wine and olive oil, then pour it over the vegetables. Toss to mix well, then spread the vegetables evenly over the tin. Cover with parchment paper and seal with foil.

Bake the vegetables in the preheated oven for about 50 minutes. Remove the tin from the oven and uncover. The vegetables should have released their juices and softened. If the mixture looks dry, add a splash of hot water. Gently mix to avoid breaking the vegetables. Taste and adjust the seasoning, if necessary.

Reduce the heat to 170°C/150°C/325°F/gas 3. Return the tin, uncovered, to the oven on a low rack and bake for a further 40 minutes, gently mixing a couple of times. The dish is ready when the juices have reduced and thickened, leaving mostly oil, and the potatoes have turned golden and started to crisp up.

Salads

CHAPTER 8

Choriatiki **Greek salad**

FROM **THE ISLANDS**

SERVES 2–4

2 ripe tomatoes (about 400g/14oz, or use cherry tomatoes)
Pinch of sugar (optional)
½ cucumber or 1 small cucumber
½ green bell pepper (about 80g/3oz) or 1 small green bell pepper, deseeded and thinly sliced
½ onion (about 80g/3oz) or 1 small onion
6–7 good-quality black olives (such as Kalamata)
60ml (2fl oz) olive oil
1 tablespoon vinegar (optional)
1½ teaspoons dried oregano
150g (5½oz) *xinomizithra* or feta
1–2 tablespoons capers, rinsed and dried
Sea salt
Fresh crusty bread, to serve

Greek salad is perhaps the most popular summer dish ordered at tavernas across Greece. Although *choriatiki* translates as 'from the village', it was invented and popularised in the tavernas of Plaka, the historic district of central Athens. As simple as it appears, the Greek salad embodies a whole science. It is a celebration of those vegetables abundant during the summer months. Juicy tomatoes, crisp cucumbers , tangy bell peppers, sweet onions and glossy black olives are crowned by chunks of salty, creamy feta and fragrant oregano leaves, then dressed with a drizzle of good olive oil – it's summer on a plate!

Greek salads really shine when the ingredients are in season and island variations incorporate local ingredients. Fresh, creamy local cheeses take on a starring role and give the salad a whole different dimension. Capers and caper leaves, samphire and distinctive olives, like the wrinkled black *throubes* from Thasos, Crete's unique tiny olives or the small pickled whole spicy green peppers they often add on Lesvos. Wild-grown purslane or fresh herbs like the small-leafed island basil, sprouting from pots and tins everywhere, or *thymbra* (wild thyme) and oregano, which add spice. All these additional touches beautifully elevate the dish on each island adding variety and making each salad unique. The best part about a Greek salad is what Greeks call *papara*: dipping good bread into the dressing and soaking up every last drop of the juices in there.

Cut the tomatoes into bite-sized pieces (or if using cherry tomatoes, cut them in half) and place in a bowl. If the tomatoes are not very sweet, sprinkle them with a pinch of sugar, mix well and let them sit for 10–15 minutes.

Peel the cucumber (unless it is very fresh). Cut the cucumber in half lengthways and slice it into chunks about 1–1.5cm (½ inch) thick. Cut the bell pepper into thin slices. Peel, halve and core the onion, then cut it into thin slices. Add the cucumber, bell pepper, onion and olives to the bowl with the tomatoes.

Mix 2 tablespoons of the olive oil with the vinegar and drizzle it over the salad. Sprinkle in 1 teaspoon of the dried oregano, season with salt and toss well.

Place the cheese on top, then spoon the capers around and over the cheese. Drizzle the remaining olive oil over the salad and sprinkle on the remaining dried oregano. Break up the cheese in the bowl. Serve immediately with fresh bread.

TIP

For the perfect Greek salad, the tomatoes should be ripe, sweet and never refrigerated. Storing tomatoes in the fridge prevents them from ripening properly and ruins their texture. If you cannot find ripe tomatoes, opt for the sweetest variety available – cherry tomatoes are a safe choice. When using larger tomatoes, as they usually do in Greece, I particularly love it when the tomato is peeled, especially if the tomatoes are thick skinned.

Salata me omo kolokithaki **Courgette salad with grapes, mint and sesame seeds**

VE GF

FROM **THE CYCLADES**

SERVES 2–4

50–400g (12–14oz) courgettes (zucchini), ideally small and very fresh
3 tablespoons fresh lemon juice
1 teaspoon honey
200g (7oz) white seedless grapes, halved if small or thinly sliced
1 spring onion (scallion), finely sliced
2–3 tablespoons chopped fresh mint
½ teaspoon lemon zest (unwaxed)
2 tablespoons toasted sesame seeds
3 tablespoons extra virgin olive oil
1 teaspoon crushed pink peppercorns (optional)
Salt and freshly ground black pepper

When courgette (zucchini) plants are in bloom on the islands, locals use both the courgettes and their flowers in various wonderful ways. This refreshing, light salad is inspired by the raw courgette salads I've enjoyed during summers on the Cycladic islands, such as Tinos and Paros, which usually feature the local small courgettes. Ideally very fresh, small courgettes yield the best results in this recipe due to their crunchiness and superior flavour. I love adding grapes to this salad because they complement the courgettes with a lovely sweetness, balancing the tangy flavours. For an extra kick, you can add a bit more lemon juice at the end along with the olive oil. You might also enjoy incorporating something spicy like a thinly sliced red chilli or some cheese, such as crumbled feta, grilled halloumi or thin shavings of Parmesan. When kept fairly plain, like in this recipe, it's a really versatile salad and makes an excellent summery side dish for grilled meat, chicken or fish.

Trim the courgettes and slice them lengthwise into ribbons using a Y-shaped vegetable peeler. Cut the courgette slices into thin matchsticks. (Alternatively, you can use a mandolin for this step.)

Combine the honey and lemon juice in a large mixing bowl and stir until the honey dissolves. Place the courgettes in the bowl with the lemon and honey mixture, then season with salt and pepper to taste. Mix well, cover the bowl and place in the fridge to marinate for 30–60 minutes.

Once marinated, drain the courgettes in a sieve (strainer) and let them sit for 5 minutes. Transfer the courgettes to a bowl and mix in the grapes, spring onions, mint, lemon zest, 1½ tablespoons of the sesame seeds and 2 tablespoons of the olive oil. Season with salt and freshly ground black pepper. Toss everything together well.

Arrange the salad on a serving platter, drizzle over the remaining olive oil and sprinkle on the remaining sesame seeds and crushed pink peppercorns, if using. Serve immediately.

Karpouzi ke peponi me tyri **Melon and watermelon salad with feta, mint, pistachios and honey**

FROM **LIMNOS**

SERVES 2–4

200g (7oz) melon (I use Galia and Cantaloupe), cut into cubes and chilled
200g (7oz) watermelon, cut into cubes and chilled
100–150g (3½–5½oz) feta, cubed
2 tablespoons unroasted pistachios
2 tablespoons extra virgin olive oil (early harvest, if possible)
2 teaspoons runny thyme honey (or any other honey)
12 small mint leaves, whole or roughly chopped
Sea salt and freshly ground black pepper

Limnos is a charming large island with a deep-rooted history in farming. Its lush landscapes yield renowned wines, cheeses, pulses and grains, all reflecting the island's rich agricultural heritage. The island hosts fields with barley and wheat, including a special local variety called *mavragani*. This unique grain produces exceptional flour used to make the island's delicious breads, rusks and traditional pasta, including *flomaria* and *trahanas*. The local cheeses are truly remarkable, crafted from the milk of sheep and goats. The renown *kaskavali, melichloro* and PDO cheeses *feta* and *kalathaki* are a testament to Limnos' commitment to quality and tradition. Thanks to Limnos' volcanic soil, the island produces a wonderful array of vegetables and fruits. It's famous for its vibrant tomatoes, flavourful melons and sweet watermelons. Among these are rare, old varieties like the anhydrous melons known as *vontones*. When unripe, these unique melons make a refreshing addition to local salads, standing in for cucumbers. The island also grows various types of watermelons, including a gourd-like variety affectionately called *alepoudes* or 'foxes' by the locals. In recent years, Limnos' thyme honey has earned international acclaim. For a refreshing summer treat, I love to blend some of the island's signature ingredients – melons, watermelons and thyme honey – with creamy feta cheese.

This simple recipe is perfect for any time of day, including breakfast. The juicy melons, sweet honey, and tangy feta come together to create a delightful flavour combination. Feel free to use any variety of melon you like; I enjoy mixing different ones for added colour and flavour. I also toss in some pistachios for a satisfying crunch and fresh mint for a burst of brightness.

Place the melon and watermelon cubes in a colander to drain any excess moisture, then arrange them on a serving platter. Scatter the feta cubes over the fruit, followed by half of the toasted pistachios. Season with sea salt and freshly ground black pepper.

Drizzle the olive oil over the salad, followed by the honey. Finish by sprinkling over the remaining toasted pistachios and chopped mint on top. Serve immediately.

Patatosalata **Potato salad with tomato, cucumber, egg and smoked mackerel**

FROM **CRETE**

SERVES 2–4

320g (11oz) potatoes suitable for boiling, left whole with skins on
1 small cucumber (such as Lebanese), cut into thin rounds
½ red onion, thinly sliced
10 baby plum tomatoes or other small tomatoes, halved
100g (3½oz) smoked mackerel, sliced
1–2 hard-boiled eggs, quartered
Pinch of dried oregano
6–8 black olives
1 tablespoon capers, drained, rinsed and dried
About 50g (1¾oz) purslane, trimmed into smaller stalks (or use lamb's lettuce, baby spinach or watercress)
Sea salt and freshly ground black pepper

FOR THE DRESSING
50ml (1¾fl oz) olive oil
1½ teaspoons wine vinegar
1½ teaspoons fresh lemon juice

Potatoes hold a special place in island cuisine, featuring in countless recipes from salads to omelettes, fritters and pies. They bring a sense of ease and comfort that everyone appreciates, with endless ways to enjoy them! In Crete, one popular way to enjoy potatoes is in a salad – quick to prepare yet satisfyingly filling, making them a perfect meal solution. Boiled potato salads are a staple, often served alongside foraged greens or hard-boiled eggs. Often, the salad is prepared simply with just tomatoes, onions and olives, or made more elaborate with ingredients such as rusks, capers, cucumber or cured fish. Personally, I love adding smoked mackerel to this potato salad; it pairs beautifully with the boiled eggs and potatoes. Often in Crete, both vinegar and lemon are used in the potato salad dressing, which is quite uncommon in traditional Greek recipes that usually use either one or the other to enhance acidity. A good-quality olive oil is essential here – I suggest an early harvest. Boiled potatoes and olive oil is a match made in heaven; potatoes are frequently used in olive oil tastings as their neutral flavour allows the rich, robust notes of the olive oil to shine through, providing a perfect medium to appreciate the oil's unique characteristics.

Place the whole potatoes in a large pan of salted water and bring to the boil over a high heat. Boil the potatoes until cooked through – the cooking time will vary depending on their size. Once cooked, drain the potatoes and leave them to cool. Once cool enough to handle, peel the skins off the potatoes and cut them into rough chunks.

Meanwhile, prepare the dressing. Mix together the olive oil, vinegar and lemon juice.

Arrange all the salad ingredients (except the eggs) on a large serving platter or toss them together in a salad bowl. Season with sea salt and freshly ground black pepper, then drizzle over the dressing. Gently toss to coat all the ingredients in the dressing.

When ready to serve, quarter the hard-boiled eggs, season with salt and pepper and nestle them on top of the salad. Serve immediately.

GREEK ISLAND CHEESES

The cheeses from the Greek islands showcase an unexpected array of diversity, defying the typical expectation centered around feta. According to European PDO law, feta can only be made from specific local breeds of sheep and goat, with a composition of at least 70% ewes' milk and no more than 30% goats' milk. This designation strictly applies to mainland Greece and includes only three islands: Evia (which geographically belongs to mainland Greece), Lesvos and Limnos. Even on Kefalonia, where exceptionally high-quality feta is produced, official PDO recognition remains elusive despite its acclaim.

The islands boast a wide range of both fresh and aged cheeses, deeply rooted in local traditions shaped by their landscapes, climates and cultural heritage. These cheeses are crafted in homes, monasteries, convents, island cooperatives and private dairies.

Predominantly made from ewes' or goats' milk, or often a blend of both, cheeses have long served as an important method for islanders to preserve their milk and showcase the diverse culinary heritage of their region. Whether enjoyed plain or incorporated into local recipes, these cheeses grace tables from breakfast to dessert.

In addition to sheep and goats found across the islands, dairy cows are also raised, particularly on islands like Tinos, Andros, Syros and Naxos, where cheesemaking thrives. These islands produce a remarkable variety of cows' milk cheeses. For instance, Syros is renowned for its San Michali cheese, reminiscent of Parmesan. Tinos offers its graviera, while both Tinos and Andros are celebrated for their distinctive ball-shaped cheese named volaki. Naxos contributes its own graviera, distinguished by a harmonious blend of cows' milk with small amounts of ewes' and goats' milk, resulting in a cheese that ages beautifully.

Fresh, creamy cheeses, usually crafted from ewes' or goats' milk, abound across the islands and are staples in daily diets. Fresh, tangy cheeses, like Skyros' xinotyri or xinomyzithra from the Cyclades and Crete, are perfect when drizzled with honey or used in salads instead of feta, or paired with fresh fruits such as watermelon or figs. Santorini's chloro cheese is enjoyed fresh, while Ikaria's kathoura, a goats' milk cheese, reveals its full potential when aged, developing rich flavours. Anthotiro and mizithra, reminiscent of ricotta and made from whey leftover from other cheeses, are both prized for their creamy texture and mild flavour when fresh. These versatile cheeses, which are also aged and dried, are cherished in cooking and baking.

Cheese-making on the islands involves traditional methods and local resources, like marble slabs or special braided baskets, which lend unique shapes to cheeses like Kimolos' kalathi and Lemnos' kalathaki. On Tinos, Petroma cheese is meticulously crafted from fresh cows' milk, with curds pressed between marble or weights to remove excess whey and achieve desired density. Unique blue cheeses are also produced, like the wonderful kariki from Tinos, aged in sealed gourds, or kopanisti (meaning 'beaten') from Mykonos and other Cycladic islands, which during the aging process, is periodically mixed or 'beaten' to encourage the development of its characteristic molds. Ancient aging techniques, such as aging in clay pots or special pits, are also employed. Serifos is known for cheeses like tyri toy lakou ('cheese of the pit') which ages for at least 3 months in a pit that is 2.5 metres deep. Island cheesemaking traditions include aging cheeses in touloumi (goat skin), like touloumotiri found on Milos, Kea and Lesvos, each offering a unique flavour profile despite sharing the same name. Anafi produces vrasto cheese, boiled in salted water and then air-dried to harden. Often herbs or other greens are incorporated into cheeses for flavour, such as the Cretan graviera with thyme or the Lazareto cheese they make in Ithaca with samphire.

Ancient methods of island cheesemaking include using staple ingredients in aging, such as wine or olive oil and local herbs. Sifnos' manoura ages in ceramic vessels with wine sediments, while Ios' xinotiri, Folegandros' gylomeni and Kos' krasotyri also derive their distinct tastes from aging in similar ways. Olive oil is used in the different variations of ladotyri (oil-cheese), which is found on many islands including Folegandros, Paros, Evia, Zakinthos, Kythira and Lesvos. On Milos island, kefalisio cheese is crafted from goats' milk, rubbed with olive oil sediment and aged on wild thyme twigs in the island's caves. Other island cheeses aged in caves include renowned gravieras from Crete and Kasos, enhancing their flavours and textures in this ideal natural environment. Although it may come as a surprise to many, France isn't the only European country producing a huge range of fantastic cheeses. Greece is certainly giving them a run for their money.

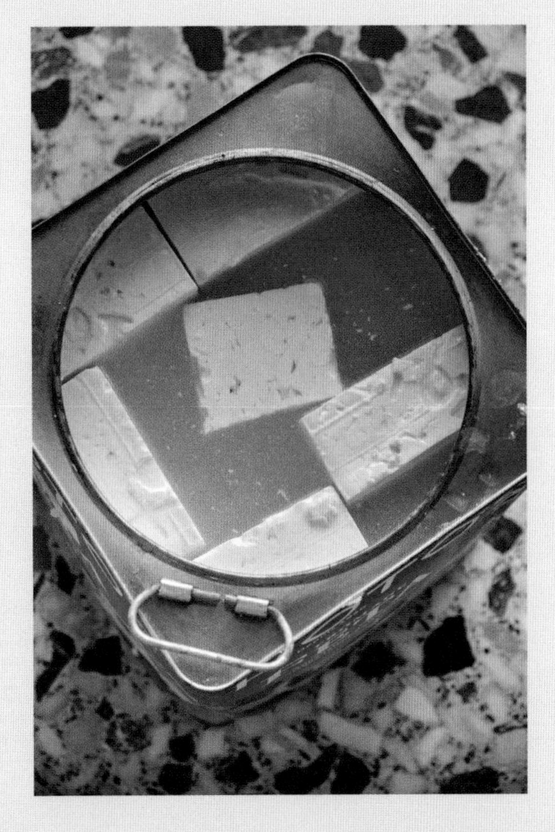

Chtapodi xidato me mavromatika **Octopus and black-eyed pea salad with capers**

FROM **PAROS AND ANTIPAROS**

SERVES 4

FOR THE OCTOPUS

- 1 octopus (around 1kg/2lb 4oz), fresh or frozen, cleaned
- 1 bay leaf
- 4 tablespoons red wine
- 4 tablespoons red wine vinegar
- 10 black peppercorns

FOR THE PRESERVED OCTOPUS

- 10 black peppercorns
- 2 bay leaves
- 1 fresh oregano sprig
- ½ teaspoon honey
- 80ml (2½fl oz) olive oil
- 80ml (2½fl oz) red wine vinegar

FOR THE SALAD

- 150g (5½oz) dried black-eyed peas or other small white beans like cannellini (about 300g/10½oz cooked weight), boiled in salted water
- 1 bay leaf
- 2 spring onions (scallions), thinly sliced on the diagonal
- 1–2 tablespoons capers, rinsed, drained and dried
- 2 tablespoons chopped fresh parsley
- 1 teaspoon dried oregano
- 3–4 tablespoons preserved sliced octopus (see above), drained
- 1½ tablespoons red wine vinegar
- 3 tablespoons olive oil
- Sea salt

One of the most iconic sights on the Greek islands is of an octopus hanging on a clothesline or hook outside a seaside taverna, drying under the strong sun and sea breeze – a common scene in Paros and Antiparos. This traditional method not only preserves the octopus but also intensifies its flavour, making it a unique and cherished ingredient in the cuisine of these islands. Whether enjoyed as part of a simple meze, grilled and served with ouzo, or featured as a main dish in a rich stew, octopus truly embodies the essence of Greek island life and its enduring traditions. In Paros and Antiparos, octopus is a staple, with one of the most beloved preparations being *xidato*, where it's preserved in vinegar. This is the simplest way to prepare octopus, allowing it to be kept in the fridge for several days. It makes for a convenient snack and a quick addition to salads and bruschettas. The quality of vinegar you use is crucial – opt for a good-quality wine vinegar to enhance the flavour of your *xidato*.

On these islands, octopus and other seafood are often paired with pulses such as *fava* (see page 40) or black-eyed peas. Black-eyed peas are a staple in the Cycladic islands and Limnos. On Limnos, a rare local variety called *aspromitika* (meaning 'white-nosed') is grown. These beans are slightly smaller and have a white eye instead of the usual black – they work great in salads. Black-eyed peas are enjoyed year-round in various recipes, frequently mixed with herbs or greens in salads. During the summer, fresh black-eyed pea pods, known as *ampelofasoula*, make a popular and simple salad. The beans are boiled and then dressed with olive oil and vinegar or lemon, or sometimes with grated (shredded) fresh tomatoes and garlic.

If the octopus is frozen, let it defrost completely and bring it to room temperature before cooking. Wash the octopus well and let it drain in a colander.

Place a heavy-based pan with a lid over a medium-high heat. Once hot, put the octopus in the pan (head side down) and add the bay leaf. As the octopus starts to release its juices, add the wine, vinegar and black peppercorns. Cover the pan immediately, reduce the heat to low and gently simmer the octopus its own juices for about 45 minutes. Check occasionally and if the pan looks too dry, add a splash of hot water. To check for doneness, insert a knife into the thickest part of the tentacles – the octopus should be tender and the knife should slide in easily. Once cooked, remove the pan from the heat and set it aside to cool. Once cooled, remove the octopus from the pan and cut it into slices.

Recipe continues overleaf

To preserve the octopus, place the slices in a large sterilised jar or glass container with a sealing lid. Taste the octopus to check if it's salty enough on its own; it often has enough natural salt and doesn't need any extra. Add the fresh black peppercorns, bay leaves and oregano to the jar with the octopus. (Discard the ones used to cook the octopus; do not reuse them.) In a separate bowl, mix the honey with the vinegar, adding a little salt if necessary, until the honey dissolves. Gradually mix in the olive oil until it's all incorporated. Pour this mixture into the jar over the octopus, ensuring it is completely submerged – if necessary, add more olive oil. Leave the octopus to marinate for up to 3 days – the longer it marinates, the better it will taste.

You can serve the preserved octopus plain as a sharing dish, drizzled with fresh olive oil and sprinkled with dried oregano, or you can use it in salads and other dishes. The remaining oil can also be used as a dressing or in other creative ways such as in a pasta dish.

FOR THE BLACK-EYED PEA SALAD

Place the black-eyed peas in a pan of salted water, then add a bay leaf. Bring to the boil over a medium heat and cook for 30 minutes or until soft. (The black-eyed peas do not require soaking, but can be boiled directly.) Once cooked, drain the peas in a colander.

Place the drained peas in a large bowl and mix together with the spring onions (scallions), capers, parsley, oregano and salt. Add in the octopus. In a separate bowl, gradually mix the vinegar into the olive oil until it's all incorporated. Pour the dressing over the salad, then gently toss to coat all the ingredients. Taste and adjust the seasoning, if necessary. Serve immediately.

Roka me aginara, liasti tomata & graviera **Rocket salad with artichokes, capers and graviera cheese**

FROM **TINOS**

SERVES 4

80g (2½oz) lettuce, shredded
60g (2oz) rocket (arugula), washed and dried
90g (3oz) artichoke hearts from a jar, drained and sliced
2 spring onions (scallions), thinly sliced
2 tablespoons capers, drained and rinsed
2 tablespoons roughly chopped fresh dill
1 tablespoon olive oil
1 teaspoon balsamic vinegar
100g (3½oz) graviera, pecorino or other hard cheese, cut into thin slivers
Sea salt

FOR THE DRESSING

30g (1oz) sun-dried tomatoes, plus 1 tablespoon oil from the jar
1 small garlic clove, peeled
60ml (2fl oz) olive oil
20ml (¾fl oz) balsamic vinegar
Sea salt and freshly ground black pepper

Artichokes feature prominently in salads on both Tinos and Crete, where artichoke production thrives. In Crete, salads often pair raw or preserved artichoke hearts with crispy lettuce and spring onions (scallions). On Tinos, artichokes are commonly combined with rocket (arugula) and local sun-dried tomatoes, as well as local hard cheese, such as *graviera*. Rocket grows wild during spring and it's one of the most commonly foraged greens, known for its distinctive peppery and slightly bitter flavour, which is more intense than that of regular cultivated rocket. Its sharp, mustard-like taste adds a lively kick to salads and other dishes like omelettes. The cheese doesn't need to be *graviera* from Tinos (although it is exported to other parts of the world). It can be any kind of *graviera* from other parts of Greece or any other hard cheese that can be thinly sliced, such as manchego, pecorino or Parmesan.

First, prepare the dressing. Place the sun-dried tomatoes, 1 tablespoon of oil from the jar and garlic in a blender or food processor. Add the olive oil and balsamic vinegar. Blitz to a paste. Season with salt and freshly ground black pepper.

Place the lettuce and rocket in a large mixing bowl, add the artichokes, spring onions, capers and dill. Season with a pinch of salt and drizzle over the olive oil and balsamic vinegar. Gently toss to coat all the ingredients in the oil.

Arrange all the salad ingredients on a serving platter and drizzle over the dressing. Scatter the slivers of cheese on top and serve immediately.

Mirmizeli **Grilled aubergine and tomato salad with olives and anchovies**

FROM **KALYMNOS**

SERVES 2–4

120g (4oz) wheat rusks (or other rusks such as barley, carob, wholewheat) or croutons made from grilled stale bread
180g (6oz) baby plum tomatoes, quartered (or use cherry tomatoes, halved)
1 small cucumber (such as Lebanese), sliced into thin rounds
1 small onion, thinly sliced and roughly chopped
1½ tablespoons capers, drained, rinsed and dried
8–10 black olives
1 teaspoon dried oregano or *thymbra* (wild thyme)
3 tablespoons roughly chopped parsley leaves
12 salted anchovy fillets in olive oil, drained
Sea salt and freshly ground black pepper

FOR THE VINAIGRETTE
1 small ripe tomato (about 180g/6oz) or cherry tomatoes
1 tablespoon red wine vinegar
60ml (2fl oz) extra virgin olive oil
Sea salt and freshly ground black pepper

Also known as The Spongers' Island, Kalymnos is nestled between Leros and Kos in the Dodecanese. This fishermen's island is renowned for its cuisine, which heavily relies on fish and seafood. Octopus features prominently in many recipes, from grilled dishes to fritters, and local fishermen are renowned divers and masters at preserving seafood, such as their famous *spinialo*. One of their stand-out local recipes is a hearty salad featuring rusks, the popular double-baked bread found throughout the islands in many forms and variations. These rusks are often used as a substitute for fresh bread and frequently appear in salads.

This salad typically includes barley rusks along with tomatoes, onions, parsley, olives and capers. It's topped with the local *kopanisti*, a creamy, aged cheese produced on the island. Grilled aubergines and salted sardines are often added, making it a perfect dish for locals to share over wine or ouzo. I usually omit the cheese but I do use salted sardines or anchovies. If you wish to incorporate cheese as well, you could add some crumbled feta. If you can't get Greek-style rusks, use stale bread or sliced fresh bread that has been grilled, cut into chunks and left to dry as it cools down. I like to make a tomato vinaigrette for this salad which is very versatile and works well on other salads.

First, make the vinaigrette. Place the tomatoes in a food processor and pulse until smooth. Strain the mixture through a sieve (strainer) into a small bowl to remove any skin and seeds. Using a whisk, mix in the vinegar. While whisking vigorously, gradually add the olive oil until incorporated. Season with sea salt and freshly ground black pepper and set aside.

Break the rusks into smaller chunks. Place the rusks in a large bowl and spoon over half of the tomato vinaigrette. Leave them to soften for 2–3 minutes. (If using croutons or grilled bread, do not soak them in the vinaigrette. When using stale bread, it depends on how dried out it is.) Add all the vegetables to the same bowl, including the capers, olives, oregano and parsley, and mix well. Gradually add half of the remaining vinaigrette while tossing the salad.

Arrange the salad on a deep serving platter, then drape the anchovy fillets on top. Drizzle the remaining vinaigrette over the salad and season with an extra grinding of black pepper, if you like.

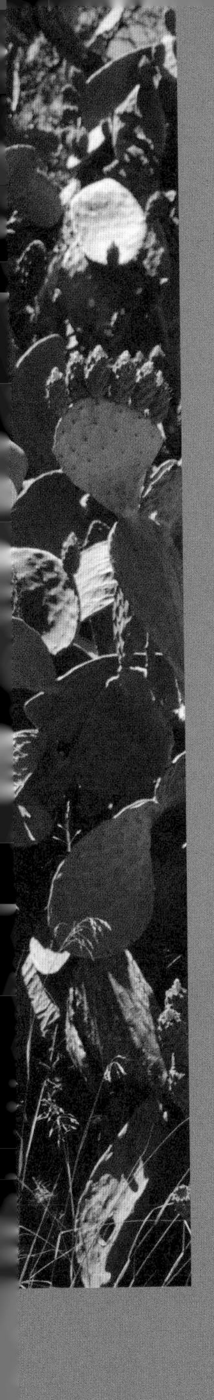

Sweet Treats

CHAPTER 9

Mamoulia **Cookies with nuts and orange blossom water**

FROM **CHIOS**

MAKES ABOUT 50

FOR THE COOKIES
80ml (2½fl oz) milk
170g (6oz) granulated sugar
170g (6oz) butter
150ml (5fl oz) olive oil
700g (1lb 8oz) plain (all-purpose) flour
2 eggs
4 tablespoons) orange juice
½ teaspoon bicarbonate of soda (baking soda)
½ teaspoon baking powder
½ teaspoon ground cinnamon
2 tablespoons *metaxa* or brandy

FOR THE FILLING
30g (1oz) almonds
30g (1oz) walnuts
½ teaspoon ground cinnamon
2 tablespoons orange blossom water

TO FINISH
Orange blossom water, for brushing or spritzing
Icing (confectioners') sugar, for coating

This stuffed cookie is prepared during Christmas on Chios, often flavoured with their local *mastiha*. A similar cookie is made in Rethymno, Crete and Limnos, where they are called *mamounia*. The versions found on the Greek islands differ slightly from Arabic ones. The dough always includes alcohol: *metaxa* (brandy) in Chios and Limnos or *tsikoudia* (grape distillate) in Crete. The filling is either chopped almonds or walnuts, or both, combined with orange blossom water. This creates a fusion of traditional *amygdalota* and *kourampiedes*, almond-based treats prepared on most islands.

This recipe was given to me by Eleftheria Fardi, a wonderful cook from Livadia on the eastern side of Chios. She was taught to make these by her uncle Stephos, a cook on ships. She makes them with olive oil and butter, then stuffs them with both almonds and walnuts. These cookies can be dusted in sugar, but I often leave half of them plain.

Gently heat the milk and sugar in a small pan, stirring until the sugar has dissolved. In a separate pan, combine the butter and olive oil. Place the pan over a low-medium heat until the butter has melted. Reduce the heat to low, pour the hot milk into the butter and oil, then stir with a silicone spatula. Next, gradually add the flour until an oily, soft dough forms. Remove the pan from the heat and let it cool for 30–40 minutes, checking occasionally and kneading to cool down.

Meanwhile, prepare the filling. Finely chop the nuts and add them to a small bowl. Mix them with cinnamon and orange blossom water, then set aside.

Place the dough in the bowl of an electric stand mixer fitted with the hook attachment. Beat the eggs in a separate bowl until frothy. Pour in the beaten eggs and mix at medium speed until well combined.

In a large jug (pitcher), combine the orange juice with the bicarbonate of soda (baking soda). It will froth and rise. Add to the dough with the baking powder and cinnamon, then knead well. The dough should be smooth and easy to form.

Preheat the oven to 180°C/160°C fan/350°F/gas 4. Line two large baking trays with parchment paper.

Shape the dough into small balls, each weighing 25g (¾ oz). Flatten each ball to form a disk. Add about ½ teaspoon of filling in the centre, bring the dough up around the filling, sealing well, and shape back into a ball. Place on the prepared trays. Leave a gap between each cookie to allow for expansion during baking.

Bake the cookies in the centre of the hot oven for 25 minutes or until lightly golden. As soon as you take them out of the oven, brush or spritz the cookies with orange blossom water. Once cool, dust each cookie with sugar until fully coated. They keep well for up to 3 weeks when stored in an airtight container.

Krema tou piatou **Vanilla custard with roasted cinnamon cherries**

FROM **AEGINA**

SERVES 6–8

FOR THE CUSTARD
1 vanilla pod (bean)
1 litre (34fl oz) whole (full-fat) milk (I use half cows' and half ewes' milk for a creamier result, but you can use regular cows' milk)
3 eggs
130g (4½oz) granulated sugar
30g (1oz) cornflour (cornstarch)
15g (½oz) butter
Ground cinnamon, to serve

FOR THE CHERRIES
400g (14oz) cherries, pitted
1 cinnamon stick
2 tablespoons *metaxa* or brandy
80ml (2½fl oz) fresh orange juice
20g (¾oz) granulated sugar

Vanilla custard – or 'plate cream' as it's fondly known in Greece – is the ultimate comfort food, right alongside rice pudding. It gets its charming name from the practice of pouring it into deep plates instead of bowls, allowing it to cool quickly. This method leaves plenty of room to sprinkle an ample amount of cinnamon on top, making every spoonful aromatic. I fondly remember my grandmother preparing both custard and rice pudding in her cosy kitchen on Aegina. She would use fresh goats' milk sourced from the convent of Agios Minas, near the ancient temple of Aphaia. Her checkered blue and white kitchen table would be covered with multiple plates, each filled with custard and rice pudding, waiting patiently to cool down. The anticipation of enjoying these treats was just as delicious as the desserts themselves!

I transform it into a proper summery dessert by adding my favourite roasted cherries on top. These cherries can be used as toppings for various treats such as ice cream, yogurt or whipped cream. They make a great addition to a cheese platter.

Using a sharp knife, split the vanilla pod (bean) lengthways and scrape the seeds into a heavy-based saucepan, then add the pod. Pour in the milk. Place the pan over a medium-low heat and gently stir until the milk begins to simmer. Remove the pan from the heat before it starts to boil. Remove and discard the vanilla pod.

In a bowl, whisk the eggs with the sugar and cornflour (cornstarch) until well combined, frothy and the sugar has dissolved. While whisking vigorously, slowly add 2–3 ladlefuls of the hot milk to the egg mixture. Once the egg mixture has warmed up, whisk it into the rest of the hot milk in the pan. Place the pan back over a low heat and whisk continuously while it thickens into a custard. Stir in the butter. Remove the pan from heat and pour the custard into individual bowls or glasses. Leave to cool to room temperature before chilling (covered) in the fridge.

To prepare the cherries, place a cast-iron or non-stick pan over a medium-high heat. Once hot, add the cherries and cinnamon stick, tossing them in the pan for 1–2 minutes. Pour in the *metaxa* and orange juice. The mixture will bubble, but keep tossing it for 1 minute. Sprinkle the sugar over the cherries and let it melt. Continue to gently toss for a further 2–3 minutes until the cherries are cooked and the sauce has reduced and thickened. This should take 3–4 minutes.

Serve the cherries warm spooned over the vanilla custard with some of their syrup and dusted with cinnamon. In the summer months, I love these cherries chilled. To chill, transfer the cherries and their syrup to an airtight container, cover and refrigerate for a few hours.

Yiaourtini **Semolina cake with yogurt, lemon and chamomile syrup**

FROM **LESVOS**

SERVES 12

200g (7oz) butter, softened, plus extra for greasing the cake mould
100g (3½oz) plain (all-purpose) flour
1 teaspoon baking powder
Pinch of salt
5 eggs at room temperature (yolks and whites separated)
150g (5oz) granulated sugar
100g (3½oz) fine semolina
1 teaspoon grated lemon zest
1 teaspoon vanilla extract
200g (7oz) Greek yogurt

FOR THE SYRUP

3 tablespoons fresh lemon juice
3–4 thin slivers lemon rind (avoiding the bitter white pith)
200g (7oz) granulated sugar
1½ tablespoons dried chamomile (or use 4–5 chamomile tea bags)

TO SERVE

Vanilla ice cream (optional)

Another island with an incredible cuisine is Lesvos, known for its fantastic local products like olive oil, olives, ouzo, seafood and dairy products, particularly their lovely cheeses and amazing sheep's milk yogurt. Yogurt is used in many local recipes, from sauces and dips to wonderful desserts such as this cake called *Yiaourtini*, named after *yiaourti*, the Greek word for yogurt. This traditional cake is made with a mix of flour and fine semolina, which absorbs syrup better and faster. If you can't get hold of semolina, simply replace it with plain (all-purpose) flour. After the cake is baked, it's drizzled with syrup infused with lemon and chamomile, both of which grow abundantly on Lesvos. I use a silicone Bundt cake mould because it's easier to add the syrup to the cake without the risk of it sticking to the mould.

Grease the base and sides of a 20cm (8 inch) silicone Bundt cake mould with a little butter.

First, make the syrup to allow it to cool to room temperature by the time the cake is ready. Place the lemon juice, lemon rind, sugar and chamomile in a saucepan over a medium heat, pour in 250ml (9fl oz) water and gently simmer for 5–6 minutes, stirring occasionally, until the sugar has dissolved. Remove from heat and let the syrup stand covered for 10 minutes. Strain the syrup through a fine sieve (strainer) and let it stand uncovered to cool to room temperature.

Preheat the oven to 180°C/160°C fan/350°F/gas 4.

Sift the flour, baking powder and salt into a large bowl. In a grease-free bowl, beat the egg whites until they form a stiff meringue. Set both aside.

In a separate bowl, beat the butter and sugar until pale and creamy. Add the egg yolks one at a time, mixing well after each addition. Stir in the lemon zest, vanilla extract and yogurt until combined. Using gentle movements, fold in the meringue with a silicone spatula. While gently mixing, gradually sprinkle in the flour mixture, followed by the semolina. Once everything is well incorporated, pour the batter into the prepared cake mould. Shake the mould to distribute the batter evenly.

Bake the cake in the hot oven for 50–60 minutes or until golden brown. Check for doneness by inserting the tip of a sharp knife; it should come out clean.

Drizzle the syrup over the cake while it's still very hot and in the mould, a tablespoon at a time, ensuring it is evenly distributed. Once all the syrup has been added, let the cake cool down to fully absorb the syrup. Remove the cake from the mould and place it on a serving platter, then serve it plain or with scoops of vanilla ice cream.

Pastafrolla **Tart with apricot jam**

FROM **CORFU**

SERVES 8

FOR THE PASTRY
200g (7oz) butter, cold and cubed, plus extra for greasing the tart pan
300g (10½oz) plain (all-purpose) flour
1 teaspoon baking powder
Pinch of salt
1 egg (yolk separated from the white)
40ml (3 tablespoons) *metaxa* or brandy
1 teaspoon grated lemon zest
90g (3oz) granulated sugar

FOR THE FILLING
450g (1lb) apricot jam (preserve), or other flavour of your choice

This tart from the Ionian islands, holds a special place in hearts all over Greece. With Venetian rule lasting from the late Middle Ages to the late eighteenth century, the islands' cuisine bears a distinctive Venetian influence, especially the cuisine of Corfu. While these tarts are popular on the Ionian islands, you'll also come across them on other islands with a strong Venetian heritage, such as Tinos and Syros.

In Corfu, this treat is especially popular. Locally known as *pastafrolla*, its name comes from the Italian *pasta frolla*, a shortcrust pastry with Venetian roots. Typically filled with jam (preserve), this tart is beautifully adorned with a decorative pastry lattice. Interestingly, similar tarts are made in Latin America, particularly in Argentina and Uruguay, where they are called *pasta frola*. Both the Greek and Latin American versions resemble the Italian *crostata* and feature the iconic checkered lattice top. As this recipe gained popularity throughout Greece, the name evolved to *pasta flora*, paying homage to its Italian origins while playfully adopting Flora, a common female name in Greece, as a charming name for a sweet pie – Flora's pie. Greek versions often include a splash of brandy, particularly *metaxa*. While apricot jam is the most common filling, you might also find variations with fig, strawberry or plum flavours.

In an electric stand mixer fitted with the paddle attachment, sift together the flour, baking powder and salt. Add the cold butter and mix on medium-low speed until the mixture resembles coarse crumbs. Add the egg yolk, *metaxa* and lemon zest. Mix at medium speed until the dough comes together, ensuring not to overmix. The dough should be soft, not sticky and easy to shape. If the dough is too sticky, add a bit more flour. If the dough is too firm, add 1 teaspoon cold water. Divide the dough in half, shape into a ball and flatten into a disc. Wrap each disc in cling film (plastic wrap) and chill in the fridge for 30 minutes.

Preheat the oven to 180°C/160°C fan/350°F/gas 4. Grease a 25–27cm (8–9 inch) tart pan or springform pan with butter.

On a lightly floured surface, roll out one half of the dough to a thickness of about 3mm (1/16 inch). Carefully line the base of the prepared pan with the rolled-out dough, neatly trimming away any excess around the edges. Spread your chosen jam evenly inside the tart case.

Roll out the second half of the dough to the same thickness, then cut it into narrow strips about 1cm (⅓ inch) wide. Place the strips over the tart case in a lattice pattern, first horizontally, then vertically. Brush the lattice and edges of the tart case with beaten egg or milk to ensure a lovely golden colour when baked.

Bake the tart on the middle rack in the hot oven for 25–30 minutes, or until the tart case is golden brown and the filling is bubbly. Allow the tart to cool completely so the filling fully sets before unmoulding and slicing.

Mosaiko **Chocolate log stuffed with vanilla ice cream and pistachios**

FROM **AEGINA**

SERVES 8–10

300g (10½oz) Petit Beurre cookies or plain tea biscuits, broken into rough pieces
150g (5oz) salted butter, melted at low temperature
150g (5oz) dark (bittersweet) chocolate, chopped
90ml (3fl oz) whole (full-fat) milk
70g (2½oz) icing (confectioners') sugar
60g (2oz) unsweetened cocoa powder, plus extra to sprinkle on top
½ teaspoon vanilla extract
30ml (2 tablespoons) *metaxa*, brandy or other liqueur such as amaretto or *fatourada* (optional)
200g (7oz) vanilla ice cream
30g (2oz) pistachios, roughly chopped and lightly toasted

When I was little, my grandmother Rena would walk me daily to Pagoudas, a famous pastry shop in the town of Aegina since 1922. There, I would get my scoop of ice cream and a slice of their delightful *mosaiko*. This easy-to-make chocolate log is a beloved treat found in many Greek freezers during summer. It's similar to English fridge cake or Italian chocolate salami. Its name, meaning 'mosaic', comes from the distinctive pattern created by the biscuits and often walnuts embedded in the log. It's made with Petit Beurre cookies, introduced to the Greek market in the early 1920s by the still-existing company Papadopoulou. These versatile cookies are widely used in many summery desserts, adding texture and providing a stable base or layers.

In my version, instead of walnuts, I use pistachios in tribute to the exceptional pistachios produced in Aegina. In Greek, pistachios are called *Phistikia Aeginis*, reflecting the island's status as the source of Greece's most famous nuts, with their bright green colour and delightful sweet flavour. Naturally, a wide array of desserts showcase the local pistachios, including caramelised versions, pralines, ice cream and baklava. Here, I use a loaf pan to assemble the dessert, layering it with vanilla ice cream and chopped pistachios for a fun, summery twist. If you're short on time, skip the ice cream layer and simply prepare the log, serving it alongside ice cream.

Line a 24 x 12cm (8 x 4 inch) loaf pan with enough parchment paper to hang over the sides. This wraps the dessert at the end and makes it easier to remove.

In a pan over a low heat (or ideally in a bain-marie), melt together the butter, chocolate, milk, icing sugar and cocoa powder, whisking until smooth and well-combined. Remove the pan from heat and stir in the vanilla extract and *metaxa*.

Place the broken cookies in a bowl, scrape in the chocolate mixture and mix until well combined. (I wear kitchen gloves for this and gently knead by hand.)

Take the ice cream out of the freezer and let it sit for a couple of minutes to soften. Press half of the cookie mixture into the lined pan to create an even layer, then spread the softened ice cream on top. Add the remaining cookie mixture on top of the ice cream, spreading it evenly and gently pressing it down. Wrap the dessert in the overhanging parchment paper and cover with cling film (plastic wrap). Chill in the freezer for at least 2–3 hours.

Remove the dessert from the freezer a couple of minutes before serving to soften for easier cutting. Sprinkle with cocoa powder and slice.

The log made with ice cream will keep in the freezer for up to 1 month. The log made without ice cream will keep for up to 3 months. Always keep it well wrapped in the freezer in both parchment paper and cling film or foil.

Pagoto yiaourti **Yogurt, honey and walnut ice cream**

FROM **SAMOTHRAKI**

MAKES ABOUT 1KG (2LB 4OZ)

- 100ml (3½fl oz) whole (full-fat) milk
- 140ml (4½fl oz) double (heavy) cream (ideally 35% fat)
- 160g (5½oz) granulated sugar
- 70g (2½oz) honey
- 4–5 drops of fresh lemon juice
- 600g (21oz) Greek-style strained yogurt (10% fat)
- 60g (2oz) walnuts, roughly chopped (optional)

Inspired by a classic Greek treat, this recipe transforms the simple trio of yogurt, honey and walnuts into a delightful ice cream. As I thought of the lush walnut trees of Samothraki in the Northern Aegean, where they are abundant, and the forest honeys and local yogurt from the island, I knew I had to transform these exquisite ingredients into an ice cream. Making your own ice cream is one of life's great pleasures, especially when you use high-quality ingredients to craft unique flavour combinations.

I've had long, enthusiastic discussions about this recipe with my friends Vicky and Igor, who own Maraboo ice-cream shop in Athens. Their tips on textures were invaluable. For the best results, use Greek-style strained yogurt that is thick, creamy and ideally full-fat (I use 10%). While an ice-cream maker gives a softer, creamier texture, you can still make delicious ice cream without one by whipping the mixture as it freezes. This ice cream is complemented by a splash of sour cherry cordial (see page 217) as well as cakes, such as *yiaourtini* (see page 174) or *mizithropita* (see page 186).

The day before, place a large metal bowl or the bowl of the ice-cream maker in the freezer, following the manufacturer's instructions. Do not remove the bowl from the freezer until you are ready to pour in the prepared ice-cream mixture.

Place the milk, cream, sugar and 35g (1½oz) of the honey in a pan over a medium-low heat. Gently whisking, heat the mixture until it begins to steam, but not boil. It should look frothy. Remove from the heat and stir for 1 minute.

Slowly whisk the yogurt into the ice-cream mixture until well combined, smooth and creamy. (You can use a blender, but I prefer to do it by hand.) Add 4–5 drops of lemon juice and mix well. Transfer the ice-cream mixture to the frozen bowl, cover with cling film (plastic wrap) and chill in the freezer for 1 hour.

If using an ice-cream maker, churn the mixture according to manufacturer's instructions. It should take around 2–3 minutes to thicken. Gradually fold the walnuts and remaining honey into the ice cream, alternating between the two.

If not using an ice-cream maker, using a handheld stick (immersion) blender or silicone spatula, beat the ice-cream mixture very well for 2–3 minutes until smooth and creamy. Cover again and return to the freezer for 30 minutes. Repeat this process every 30 minutes for the next 2–3 hours, returning the ice cream to the freezer until it thickens to the desired texture. The final time you mix the ice cream (it should have mostly thickened), fold in the walnuts and remaining honey, alternating between the two, until fully incorporated in the ice cream.

Transfer the ice cream to an airtight container and return it to the freezer for a couple of hours to firm up further.

CHIOS MASTIHA:
a Greek agricultural treasure

Nestled in the charming villages of southern Chios Island, the mastic tree (Pistacia lentiscus var. Chia) flourishes, bestowing upon the world a treasure as ancient as the land itself – Chios mastiha. For over 2,500 years, this prized natural resin has been harvested exclusively from the mastic trees of the Mastihochoria (Mastic Villages), earning Chios the title of its birthplace.

The use of Chios mastiha dates back to ancient Greece. Revered for its aromatic allure and medicinal value, mastiha was esteemed by ancient civilisations and traded across the Mediterranean, adorning religious ceremonies and enriching the realms of perfumery, incense and medicine.

Throughout time, Chios mastiha has been intertwined with the island's destiny and prosperity. In the medieval era, the Venetians established regulations to oversee its production and trade. The Genoese, renowned for their commercial prowess, furthered its prominence during their occupation of Chios, elevating it to a cornerstone of the island's economy. Under Ottoman rule, mastiha continued to thrive, becoming an integral part of Ottoman cuisine and medicine.

The significance of mastiha to the island is celebrated in folklore, art and literature, a testament to its legacy as one of Greece's most cherished agricultural treasures. While the mastic tree primarily finds its home in this unique micro-climate of southern Chios, its allure extends to other regions of the Mediterranean and the Middle East. Yet, the production of authentic Chios mastiha remains the exclusive domain of the island, where the ideal climate and traditional cultivation methods converge to yield unparalleled quality.

To extract mastiha, tiny cuts are made in the bark of the mastic tree during the summer season, enabling the resin to seep out and form into droplets upon solidification. This meticulous process yields a resin with a subtly sweet taste of pine, accentuated by undertones of citrus and floral. Chios mastiha has extensive application in Greek cuisine, enhancing the flavour of desserts, baked goods and beverages, as well as savoury dishes. It is a cornerstone ingredient in many traditional recipes, such as the famous mastiha-infused liqueur and ice cream.

Chios mastiha is no mere culinary delight; it is a symbol of cultural heritage. Revered by ancient healers like Hippocrates and Dioscorides, it is still held in high esteem for its health benefits, from digestive aid to anti-microbial and skin-soothing properties.

In the serene groves of Chios, the ritual of mastiha cultivation unfolds each passing season. Men and women of all ages partake in this labour of love, preserving not just a tradition, but a way of life. With each delicate incision and meticulously gathered droplet or 'tear', they honour the past and ensure a legacy for the future. Today, Chios mastiha stands as a beacon of authenticity and quality, recognised by the European Union with Protected Designation of Origin (PDO) status.

Galaktoboureko **Custard pie with lemon and thyme syrup**

FROM **NAXOS**

SERVES 10–12

FOR THE CUSTARD

3 eggs, at room temperature
150g (5oz) caster (superfine) sugar
1 heaped teaspoon grated lemon zest
100g (3½oz) fine semolina (or use 10g/⅓ oz cornstarch)
1 litre (34fl oz) whole (full-fat) milk
1 vanilla pod (bean) or 1 teaspoon vanilla extract
1 teaspoon butter

FOR ASSEMBLING

1 x 500g (17½oz) packet ready-made filo (phyllo) pastry
180g (6oz) butter, melted and clarified, plus extra for greasing

FOR THE SYRUP

400g (14oz) granulated sugar
2–3 fresh thyme sprigs
Zest of 1 lemon, thinly peeled with a peeler
1 tablespoon fresh lemon juice

TO SERVE

Ground cinnamon, for dusting
Fresh berries (optional)

Galaktoboureko is a cherished Greek delicacy, adored across the country and found in pastry shops and festive gatherings alike. Among Greece's delightful array of milk and custard pies, this one truly reigns supreme. The historic village of Chalki on Naxos, once the island's main town, is located in its most fertile region, right at its centre. This area is renowned for its expansive olive and citron groves – citrons that are used to produce local distillates. The town itself is beautifully preserved, with its charming neoclassical mansions, quaint shops, and cosy cafes. One such café, now known as *Spitiko Galaktoboureko* (Homemade Galaktoboureko), has been serving this legendary dessert for decades. Despite several name changes over the years, the recipe has been preserved and lovingly prepared each day. The *galaktoboureko* here is often served warm, drenched artfully in syrup to maintain a crispy outside and a juicy inside.

In my version of this classic treat, I've added lemon to the syrup and balanced the sweetness just right. To enhance the syrup, I've infused it with a hint of thyme, capturing the essence of the island's thyme-scented breezes and adding a delightful herbal note. This touch brings a bit of Naxos' aromatic charm to every bite!

First, make the syrup to allow it to cool to room temperature by the time the pie is ready. Pour 320ml (11fl oz) water into a saucepan, then add the lemon juice, lemon zest, sugar and thyme. Bring to the boil and then bubble over a medium heat for 4 minutes, stirring occasionally until the sugar has dissolved. The syrup should be thick enough to lightly coat the back of a spoon – this ensures it will soak into the layers of filo pastry without making the pie too soggy. Remove the pan from heat and let it stand, covered, for 10–15 minutes. Strain the syrup through a fine sieve (strainer) and let it stand uncovered to cool to room temperature.

Brush the base and sides of a deep, 35 x 25cm (14 x 10 inch) ovenproof dish with a little melted butter and set aside.

In a bowl, using a whisk or an electric stand mixer, beat the eggs with the sugar until pale and creamy. While whisking continuously, first add the lemon zest and then gradually add the semolina until the mixture is smooth and creamy. Gradually mix in 200ml (7fl oz) of the milk until fully incorporated.

Pour the remaining 800ml (28fl oz) of the milk into a large, heavy-based saucepan. Using a sharp knife, slit open the vanilla pod and scrape off the seeds, adding them to the milk. (If using vanilla extract, simply add it to the milk.) Heat the milk until just before it starts to simmer, then immediately remove it from the heat. Let it cool down for a minute, stirring occasionally.

Refresh the egg mixture by giving it a quick stir, then carefully start pouring a bit of the hot milk into the egg mixture, one tablespoon at a time, while whisking vigorously. Do this slowly to avoid scrambling the eggs. Once half the milk is incorporated, pour the egg mixture back into the saucepan with the remaining hot milk. Over a medium-low heat, stir continuously until the mixture starts to bubble and it begins to thicken, about 2–3 minutes. Remove the pan from the heat, stir in the butter, cover with cling film (plastic wrap) so that it is touching the custard to prevent it from drying out, and set aside.

Preheat the oven to 180°C/160°C fan/350°F/gas 4.

Divide the filo pastry sheets into two piles – half will be used for the base of the pie, while the other half will be for the top. Lay the filo pastry sheets flat on a clean work surface and keep them covered with a damp dish towel to prevent them from drying out.

Lay the first sheet of filo pastry in the baking dish, allowing any excess to hang over the sides, then brush it with melted butter. Continue layering the sheets crosswise and buttering each one until you have used half of the filo sheets set aside for the base. Fold the remaining sheets in half or as needed to cover the base of the dish and place them this way buttering them each time. Brush the top sheet with butter and pour over the prepared custard, smoothing it out nicely with a spatula. Fold the overhanging pastry inwards over the top of the custard.

Now use the remaining filo sheets set aside for the top. Place the first sheet folded in half (or as needed to fit the dish), covering the custard, then brush with butter. Place the next sheet similarly, always brushing each layer with butter. For the final three sheets, place them in a single layer, unfolded, allowing the excess pastry to hang over the sides, crosswise on top of each other. Brush each layer with butter. Fold in the excess pastry and use a silicone spatula to push it down around the sides of the pan to seal the pie.

Score the pie into 12 portions (or fewer larger portions, if preferred). Pour over any remaining melted butter and brush it evenly across the top.

Bake the pie on a low rack in the hot oven for 50–60 minutes, or until dark golden and crispy.

As soon as the pie comes out of the oven, while it is still very hot, slowly spoon the syrup over the surface of the pie, ensuring it is evenly distributed and allow it all to be absorbed. Let the pie stand until all the syrup is fully absorbed and it has cooled down.

Serve the pie lukewarm or completely cool. Sprinkle over a little ground cinnamon, if you like, and it's also great with some fresh berries on the side.

Mizithropita **Baked cheesecake with Muscat poached peaches**

FROM **PAROS**

SERVES 8

FOR THE PEACHES

4 ripe but firm peaches (around 680g/1lb 8oz)
750ml (25fl oz) sweet Muscat of Samos wine or any sweet floral white wine
80g (2½oz) demerara sugar or granulated brown sugar
1 vanilla pod (bean), split in half and seeds scraped out
1 small rosemary sprig
2 thin slivers lemon zest (unwaxed)
1 cinnamon stick

FOR THE CHEESECAKE

1 teaspoon butter, for greasing the pan
1kg (2lb 4oz) fresh *mizithra*, *anthotiro* or ricotta
80g (2½oz) icing (confectioners') sugar
4 eggs
Zest of 1 small lemon (unwaxed)
1 teaspoon baking powder
60g (2oz) fine semolina

This refreshing and summery dessert is inspired by a traditional recipe from Paros called *mizithropita*. It's a type of baked cheesecake made with *mizithra*, a fresh and creamy cheese with a mild flavour similar to ricotta. Variations of this recipe can also be found on other islands, such as Sifnos, where it is known as *melopita*.

In my twist on the classic recipe, I've added peaches poached in one of my favourite dessert wines, Muscat of Samos, which has a distinctive aroma and honeyed sweetness. The peaches and their syrup infuse the cake, making it perfect for summer. I love serving this cake with an extra poached peaches on the side, drizzled with additional syrup. The peaches can also be enjoyed on their own as a light summer treat, perfect for serving chilled with a glass of wine or as a topping for yogurt or ice cream. Any leftover syrup can also be used in various ways including cocktails.

First, prepare the peaches. Slice each peach in half and remove the stone (pit). Gently score a cross into the skin of each peach. Bring a large pan of water to the boil and prepare a bowl of iced water. Blanch the peaches, skin side down, in the boiling water for about 40–50 seconds and then transfer them straight into the iced water. Once cooled, remove the peaches and peel off the skins.

Place the wine, sugar, vanilla, rosemary, lemon zest and cinnamon stick in a wide, deep pan with a well-fitting lid. Place it over a medium heat and stir until the sugar has dissolved. Gently place the peach halves, cut side down, in a single layer in the poaching liquid, ensuring they are fully submerged. If needed, add more wine or water to cover. Bring the liquid to a gentle simmer, but do not let it boil – this will make the peaches mushy. Simmer the peaches for 10 minutes, turning them occasionally to ensure even cooking. They should be fork-tender but not too soft or falling apart. Remove the peaches from the syrup and allow both the syrup and the peaches to cool down. If the syrup is too loose, you can reduce it by boiling it down a few minutes longer. It will thicken further as it cools.

Cut 300g (10½oz) of the poached peaches into small pieces. (The rest will be used to decorate, so either cut them into thin slices or small dice.)

Preheat the oven to 180°C/160°C fan/350°F/gas 2. Generously grease a 24cm (9 inch) springform cake pan with butter.

Drain any excess liquid from the cheese, place it in a large bowl and cream well using a potato masher or fork. Add the icing sugar, mixing with a silicone spatula until well combined. Add in 150ml (5fl oz) of the cooled poaching syrup and mix well until fully combined. Fold in the peach pieces.

In a separate bowl, beat the eggs using a handheld mixer until very frothy and stiff. Mix in the lemon zest and baking powder. Fold the egg mixture into the cheese and peach mixture using a silicone spatula until just combined. While whisking continuously, gradually add in the semolina. Transfer the cheesecake mixture to the prepared tin and even it out with the spatula.

Bake the cheesecake on a low rack in the hot oven for about 1 hour, or until golden on top. While it's very hot, drizzle the cheesecake with 4 tablespoons of the reserved poaching syrup. Once it has cooled down, remove the cheesecake carefully from the pan and garnish with the reserved poached peaches.

Serve the cheesecake drizzled with some extra syrup for a delightful summery treat!

Vrahakia me Mantoles **Salted caramelised almonds covered in dark chocolate**

FROM **KEFALONIA**

MAKES ABOUT 50

200g (7oz) untoasted almonds with skins on
100g (3½oz) granulated sugar
½ teaspoon fine sea salt
330g (12oz) good-quality dark (bittersweet) chocolate, coarsely chopped
10g (⅓oz) butter

If you visit a pastry shop on cosmopolitan Greek islands like Syros, Chios, Corfu, or Kefalonia, you'll undoubtedly come across *vrahakia*. These foil-wrapped treats, often chilled in a fridge during the warmer months, are known as 'little rocks' in Greek. Their charmingly rugged appearance, with whole almonds hidden beneath a bumpy layer of chocolate, makes them look like tiny boulders.

Almond trees thrive on the Greek islands. In particular, Kefalonia is full of almond trees and almonds feature prominently in many traditional treats such as *amigdalopita* (almond pie), *mantolato* (nougat) and *mantoles* (caramelised almonds). In Kefalonia, *mantoles* are usually red: a natural red dye derived from a kind of seaweed that was added to the melting sugar, along with cinnamon and bitter almond essence. Nowadays, food colouring is primarily used. At Kappatos, an old pastry shop in the port of Argostoli, the capital of Kefalonia, you can find a wide array of almond treats, including *vrahakia*.

For *vrahakia*, almonds are typically toasted and then covered in either dark or milk chocolate. I prefer dark chocolate. Inspired by the Kefalonian *mantoles*, I caramelise the almonds before coating them in chocolate for extra flavour and crunch. I keep the almonds simple by adding just a touch of sea salt to the caramel – it perfectly balances the bitterness of the dark chocolate, sweetness of the caramel and toasted flavour of the almonds. These little rock-shaped treats are hard to resist!

Line a large metal tray with parchment paper.

Heat a wide pan over a medium-high heat. Add the almonds and toast them for 1 minute. Reduce the heat to medium-low and toast the almonds for a further 1 minute. Sprinkle the sugar over the almonds, followed by the salt, and allow the sugar to melt, which takes 2–3 minutes. Gently stir with a silicone spatula to ensure the almonds evenly caramelise and prevent them from burning. Once the caramel looks shiny and golden, immediately remove the pan from the heat.

Spoon clusters of the almonds onto the prepared tray, leaving a gap between each one. (If they do stick together, break them apart later.) Allow to cool until the caramel hardens, which takes about 20 minutes.

Meanwhile, melt the chocolate with the butter in a bain-marie or microwave, stirring until smooth and shiny. Working in small batches, submerge the almond clusters in the chocolate until fully coated, but don't let them sit in there too long. Using two spoons, transfer the coated almond clusters back onto the tray, leaving a gap between each one. Place the tray in the fridge to chill for at least 2–3 hours.

When stored in an airtight container in the fridge, they will keep well for up to 2 weeks.

SWEET DELIGHTS
On the Ferries

When travelling by ferry within Greece, particularly on routes that make a stop on Syros island, you are likely to encounter vendors who briefly enter the boat as it docks at the port. Typically men and always dressed in old-school white uniforms, they sell traditional sweets called halvadopites and loukoumia, stacked in big baskets. These vendors walk through the decks offering passengers a taste of these local delicacies to enjoy on their journey.

Halvadopites, also known as nougat pies, are a beloved Greek treat. Prepared mostly on Chios and the Cycladic islands, Syros is the most renowned for these sweet delights. Delicate unsweetened wafers embrace a rich blend of honey, sugar and typically almonds. These round flat treats are always exceptionally fresh, boasting a soft yet slightly chewy texture and delightful nutty flavour. Each halvadopita is lovingly wrapped in vibrant, intricately patterned paper, evoking a sense of nostalgia and charm, and making them an ideal gift or souvenir for travellers.

Loukoumia, known internationally as Turkish delight, has a storied history in Greece, with various regions producing their unique versions. They are particularly celebrated in Syros and Chios. These colourful, gelatinous sweets are made from a simple mixture of sugar, water and cornflour (cornstarch), and are often flavoured with rosewater, mastiha, bergamot or other citrus. They are typically coated in powdered sugar to prevent them from sticking together and they sometimes contain nuts, usually almonds or pistachios, for added texture and flavour.

Buying these sweets directly from the islands' famed confectioners on a ferry, often accompanied by the sound of the sea and the bustling atmosphere onboard, is a timeless experience that I hope will forever be preserved. These are more than just another treat; they are a piece of the islands' cultural heritage, which makes every ferry journey more exciting and a little sweeter.

Svinghi **Puffy pastry balls**

FROM **PATMOS AND SYMI**

MAKES ABOUT 30

FOR THE DOUGH
110g (3¾oz) butter
¼ teaspoon salt
20g (⅔oz) caster (superfine) sugar
160g (5½oz) plain (all-purpose) flour
¾ teaspoon vanilla extract
4 eggs, at room temperature

FOR FRIED SVINGHI
Oil, for frying
Cinnamon sugar (mix 4 tablespoons sugar with 2 tablespoons ground cinnamon, optional)
Honey (optional)
Ground cinnamon (optional)
Ground walnuts (optional)

FOR BAKED SVINGHI
Fresh fruit, such as strawberries or other berries, nectarines, figs, plums and apricots
Icing (confectioners') sugar
Quick lemony cream cheese filling (see below)

FOR THE QUICK LEMONY CREAM CHEESE FILLING
250g (9oz) fresh *mizithra* or ricotta
40g (1½oz) icing (confectioners') sugar
2 teaspoons finely grated lemon zest (unwaxed)
1 teaspoon fresh lemon juice
1 teaspoon vanilla extract

Svinghi are the island version of *loukoumades*, the airy, crispy fried puff pastry balls or rings drizzled with honey and sprinkled with cinnamon. The island variety, known as *svinghi*, includes eggs and butter in the dough, making them similar to French *beignets* or *choux* pastry and their Sicilian cousins, *sfingi*, with which they share their name.

Svinghi are typically fried and then drizzled with honey, soaked in honey syrup, or rolled in sugar and cinnamon. These kinds of treats are traditionally prepared around carnival time and are particularly popular on the Greek islands of Patmos, Chios, Symi, and Leros. Besides the fried version, *svinghi* can also be baked and filled with cream, praline, custard, lemon curd, fruit, nuts, or any filling you fancy. While sweet *svinghi* are common, they can also be made savoury, usually with cheese. They are easy and quick to make, and absolutely delicious!

To prepare the svinghi dough, put the butter, salt, sugar and 250ml (9fl oz) water in a saucepan and place it over a low heat. Once the butter has melted and sugar has dissolved, gradually add the flour while mixing with a silicone spatula until fully incorporated. Return the pan to the heat and continue stirring for 2 minutes to cook out any raw flour. The mixture should look pale and feel soft and smooth. Transfer the dough to a large mixing bowl and allow it to cool for 5 minutes.

Using an electric stand mixer, mix the cooled dough at low speed for 2–3 minutes, then start adding the eggs one at a time, making sure each one is fully incorporated before adding the next. The dough should be thick, soft, and elastic, but not sticky. Transfer the dough to a piping (pastry) bag.

For fried svinghi, place a heavy-based pan over a medium-high heat. Pour enough oil into the pan to submerge the svinghi fully. When the oil is hot (ideally around 180°C/350°F – test with a small piece of dough), pipe out small balls of dough about the size of a cherry and fry for about 4 minutes, or until puffed and golden, stirring them as they fry for even cooking. Fry in batches of 6 or 7 balls, depending on size of the pan. Using a slotted spoon, transfer the svinghi to a platter lined with paper towels to drain.

To serve, you have a couple of options. While the svinghi are still hot, roll them in cinnamon sugar until well coated. Alternatively, place the svinghi on a plate and drizzle over some honey, sprinkle on some cinnamon and, if desired, scatter over some ground walnuts.

Recipe continues overleaf

For baked svinghi, first make the quick lemony cream cheese, place the cheese in a fine sieve (strainer) and let it stand for 10 minutes to drain any excess moisture. Pat the cheese dry with paper towels and place it in a bowl. Mix the cheese until smooth. Add the sugar, lemon zest, lemon juice and vanilla extract, then mix until well combined and fluffy. You can use a handheld mixer for this. Cover and store in the fridge until ready to use.

Preheat the oven to 180°C/160°C fan/350°F/gas 4. Line a baking tray with parchment paper.

Pipe out small balls of dough about the size of a cherry onto the baking tray, leaving a small distance between each one as they will puff up. Bake in the hot oven for 25–30 minutes or until golden and puffed up. Do not open the oven to check until at least 20 minutes of the cooking time has passed. Place the svinghi on a cooling rack. Cut a small slit in the upper side, about one-third of the way down. This allows the steam to escape so they cool down faster and dry out ahead of filling.

Transfer the filling to a piping (pastry) bag and pipe some into each puff. Slice some strawberries, berries, nectarines or other fruit and gently place a couple of pieces inside the stuffed puffs. Sprinkle with icing (confectioners') sugar before serving.

Loli **Pumpkin cake with orange and honey**

FROM **SIFNOS**

600g (20oz) pumpkin (or butternut squash), peeled and grated (shredded)
Pinch of salt
100g (3½oz) self-raising flour
100g (3½oz) fine semolina
120g (4oz) icing (confectioners') sugar
½ teaspoon baking powder
30g (1oz) toasted sesame seeds, finely ground in a food processor
1 teaspoon ground cinnamon
¼ teaspoon ground cloves
80g (2½oz) currants
180ml (6½fl oz) sunflower oil, plus extra for greasing the pan
170ml (6fl oz) orange juice
2 tablespoons *metaxa* or brandy
1 teaspoon vanilla extract
2 teaspoons orange zest (unwaxed)
30g (1oz) untoasted sesame seeds
Honey or agave syrup, to serve

In Greek slang, *loli* means crazy. On Sifnos, an island known for its culinary traditions, that's what they call their delightful pumpkin cake. The locals affectionately refer to it this way because the recipe uses so many ingredients and has so many variations that it's absolutely crazy! While the list of ingredients might seem extensive, they are mostly common pantry staples, such as oil, spices, currants and sesame seeds.

Pumpkins are easy to grow on the islands. Locals make good use of them as they can be cooked in many different ways and store well for a long time. Many traditional island recipes feature pumpkin in sweet dishes, such as pies and pasties like *kolopia* from Antiparos or simply baked with cinnamon sugar and currants like *feloudia* from Limnos, or made into a spoon sweet like *koufeto* from Milos. *Loli* is quite special because it's a very light dessert, low in sugar and vegan. It has an unusual yet pleasant texture – almost creamy – and versions of it remind me of *karpouzopita*, the watermelon cake made on Cycladic islands such as Ios and Folegandros.

Loli is a an easy-to-make cake that's both healthy and delicious. Traditionally, it's served drizzled with honey and lightly dusted with cinnamon. For an extra treat, enjoy it with a scoop of vanilla ice cream or yogurt ice cream on the side.

Place the grated (shredded) pumpkin in a colander and mix it with the salt. Let it stand for 30–40 minutes to draw out any excess moisture.

In a bowl, combine all the dry ingredients: the flour, semolina, icing sugar, baking powder, ground toasted sesame seeds, ground cinnamon and ground cloves. Add in the currants and stir to coat them in the flour mixture.

In a large bowl, combine all the wet ingredients: the oil, orange juice, metaxa and vanilla extract, and mix well. Gradually pour these wet ingredients into the dry ingredients while mixing with a silicone spatula. Once everything is well incorporated, gradually stir in the pumpkin.

Preheat the oven to 180°C/160°C fan/350°F/gas 4. Grease a 30cm (10 inch) baking dish with a little oil.

Scrape the pumpkin mixture into the prepared dish and spread it out evenly using a silicone spatula. Scatter over the untoasted sesame seeds.

Bake in the hot oven for 55 minutes or until golden. The cake will be a bit wobbly as soon as it comes out of the oven, but it will set as it cools. Leave to cool completely before slicing and serving.

Patsavouropita **Filo pie with orange syrup**

FROM **LEROS**

SERVES 10–12

FOR THE SYRUP

250g (9oz) granulated sugar
150ml (5fl oz) fresh orange juice
4 teaspoons fresh lemon juice
Rind of 1 orange (unwaxed), cut into thin slivers (avoid the bitter white pith)
1 tablespoon orange blossom water (optional)

FOR THE PIE

5 eggs
200g (7oz) granulated sugar
250g (9oz) Greek yogurt
1½ teaspoons baking powder
1½ teaspoons vanilla extract
1 teaspoon grated orange zest
310ml (10½fl oz) sunflower oil
Butter, for greasing the pan
450g (1lb) store-bought thin filo (phyllo - *filo kroustas*)

TO SERVE

Vanilla ice cream, yogurt ice cream or *mastiha* ice cream (optional)

Nestled in the northern Dodecanese between Patmos and Kalymnos, Leros retains its pristine charm via a landscape with a tranquil yet mysterious atmosphere, reminiscent of the sanctuary dedicated to the goddess Artemis in Greek mythology. The island's long, diverse history, stretching from ancient times to the Second World War, is reflected in the ruins and buildings scattered across its terrain. On Leros, local desserts are a testament to the island's culinary heritage. You'll find delightful staples like *soumada*, a refreshing almond cordial; *pougakia*, small pastry pouches filled with almonds; *svigi* and *xerotigana*, crispy pancakes drizzled with honey. These treats are lovingly made at the island's most renowned pastry shop, To Paradosiako, located in the picturesque port of Agia Marina. Among these offerings, the most popular is *patsavouropita*, a pie introduced just a few decades ago by To Paradosiako. This dessert is not only a joy to eat, but an entertaining and pleasantly messy one to make.

The name *patsavouropita* comes from the Greek words *patsavoura* (rag) and pita (pie), reflecting the unique preparation method. Instead of neatly layering the filo (phyllo) dough, it's scrunched or crumpled, resembling rags. This unconventional approach creates an intriguing texture. Once baked, the pie is soaked in a fragrant orange syrup, which I enhance with a touch of orange blossom water for an extra aromatic dimension. The pie is usually served with a scoop of ice cream on the side.

First, prepare the syrup to allow it to cool to room temperature before the cake is ready. Combine the sugar, orange juice, lemon juice and orange rind in a saucepan, then pour in 150ml (5fl oz) water. Bring the mixture to a boil, then simmer for 10–15 minutes until the syrup reaches a slightly thicker consistency (it will thicken further as it cools). Remove the pan from the heat and allow it to cool completely. Once cooled, strain the syrup, reserving the orange rinds. Stir in the orange blossom water, if using. If desired, thinly slice the orange rinds into strings (to use later to garnish the top of the cake) and set aside.

To make the batter, using a handheld electric mixer, beat the eggs in a bowl for 2–3 minutes until pale and frothy. Gradually add the sugar while continuously mixing. Add the yogurt one spoonful at a time, mixing well after each addition. Next, add the baking powder, vanilla extract and orange zest. Slowly pour in the oil while continuously mixing until well combined. The mixture should be pale, creamy and fluffy.

Preheat the oven to 170°C/150°C fan/325°F/gas 3. Grease a 24cm (8 inch) springform cake pan with butter.

Recipe continues overleaf

Submerge the first filo sheet in the batter for a couple of seconds, treating it like a rug that you want to roughly cover in the mixture. (You can wear kitchen gloves for this, if you prefer.) Once the filo is moist, immediately remove it (otherwise it will fall apart) while very gently scrunching it lengthwise, to resemble a damp kitchen cloth. Avoid pressing too much as this will strain the filo and make the pie dense. Don't worry if the filo sheet isn't damp everywhere – it will moisten fast once the rest of the filo sheets are added. Also, to ensure you have enough batter for all the filo sheets, don't over-saturate the first ones as they may soak it all up and there won't be enough later. Fit the scrunched filo into one side of the pan. Continue scrunching the rest of the filo sheets into the pan, arranging them side by side, until full and all the batter and filo have been used. If you have any cake batter left, pour it over evenly or wherever the filo looks dry.

Bake the pie on a low rack in the hot oven for 35–40 minutes or until golden and risen. Remove the pie from the oven and start pouring the cooled syrup, one spoonful at a time, over the top until it is moist. To help the syrup infuse the pie, poke small holes randomly over the surface using a skewer or long toothpick. Evenly pour the syrup over the hot pie and leave to soak and cool down a bit, which will take about 20 minutes. I usually wait for it to cool completely before cutting it to ensure better slices. Serve with a scoop of vanilla ice cream on the side or it pairs beautifully with yogurt ice cream or *mastiha* ice cream.

Extras

CHAPTER 10

Kaparosalata **Caper and onion chutney**

FROM **SIFNOS**

150g (5½oz) capers
2 tablespoons olive oil
800g (1lb 12oz) onions, roughly chopped
2 bay leaves
2 small thyme sprigs
60ml (2fl oz) cider vinegar
120ml (4fl oz) sweet white wine (I use sweet Muscat from Samos, but any sweet floral wine can be used)
1 teaspoon runny honey (thyme honey works great here)
Salt and freshly ground black pepper

Capers thrive during the summer, growing wild on all the Greek islands. Every part of the plant is used, from the rounded leaves and flower buds (commonly known as capers) to the fruit (caper berries). These parts are picked in early summer, with the berries harvested later, and preserved in brine or packed with sea salt. On the Cycladic islands, where capers are everywhere you look, the larger, fluffier caper buds are salted and sun-dried. These special capers are hard to find outside the islands, but locals use them in traditional recipes like *kaparosalata*.

A dish popular on Tinos, Syros, Kythnos and Sikinos, *kaparosalata* showcases a garlicky caper dip with boiled potatoes. However, on Sifnos, an island particularly famous for its capers, the recipe takes on a different approach. *Kaparosalata* here is more like a chutney, cooked with onions and plenty of vinegar, served both warm and chilled. Its strong flavour makes it an ideal meze for the local raki (grape distillate). It's usually served as a dip with bread but also pairs perfectly with cheeses, cold cuts and grilled meats. If you can source dried capers, first rehydrate them in water, changing the water a few times, and then boil them a couple of times before use. Due to their scarcity, I've adapted the recipe using the more commonly found jarred capers.

Drain the capers and rinse them well under cold running water. Place the capers in a bowl, cover with fresh water and leave to soak for 30 minutes, changing the water 4 or 5 times throughout the process.

Once soaked, blanch the capers in boiling water for 2 minutes. Drain and then dry them on a clean dish towel. Leave to cool to room temperature.

Place a large, deep frying pan (skillet) over a medium heat. Heat the olive oil and then add the onions, bay leaves and thyme sprigs. Season with a little salt and sauté, gently stirring, until the onions are very soft and most of the liquid has evaporated. Add the capers to the pan and sauté, stirring, for a further 2 minutes

Pour in the vinegar and stir until most of the liquid has evaporated. Next, add in the wine and simmer over a very low heat for 40–45 minutes, or until the liquid has completely gone and the onions have caramelised. Remove the pan from the heat, discard the bay leaves and thyme sprigs, then stir in the honey. Taste and adjust the seasoning, if necessary, then leave the chutney to cool. Once cool, transfer the chutney to a sterilised jar.

When stored in the fridge, this chutney will keep for several months.

Beltes **Homemade tomato sauce or paste**

FROM **MILOS**

MAKES 400ML (14FL OZ) OF TOMATO SAUCE OR 200ML (7FL OZ) OF TOMATO PASTE

1.2kg (2lb 11oz) very ripe tomatoes
½ teaspoon fleur de sel or 1–2 teaspoon olive oil (optional)

Most islands, especially small ones like the Cyclades, grapple with water scarcity, yet they nurture crops traditionally without irrigation, known as *anydra* (anhydrous). This unique method yields smaller but exceptionally sweet produce, bursting with unforgettable flavours and aromas. Local treasures, such as tomatoes, cucumbers, courgettes (zucchini), pumpkins, melons, aubergines (eggplants), watermelons, grapes, figs, and more, thrive mostly on nutrients from the soil. The islands are particularly famous for their local tomato varieties, especially those grown naturally and mostly anhydrous, finding ideal conditions to flourish on volcanic islands. These tomatoes tend to be smaller in size, flavourful, sweet and very aromatic. Notably famous are the varieties from Santorini, Milos and Nisyros.

Traditional island cooking is all about preserving, and the tomato is one of the stars of this culinary tradition. Grown in abundance, tomatoes – fresh or preserved – are one of the basic ingredients in Greek cooking. They are sun-dried, preserved as pulp, sauce or paste for winter use, pickled, and even made into jams (preserves) and spoon sweets. On Milos, a volcanic island with stunning beaches, tomato preservation stands out. The island boasts two main varieties: the small *bournela*, resembling the local Santorini tomato, and the slightly larger *rousiki*, similar to the Roma tomato. These plum tomato varieties are perfect for making sauces and particularly paste. During summer, locals collect ripe tomatoes and prepare paste using the sun instead of the stove. They separate the skins and seeds from the pulp, season the pulp with sea salt, and place it in a clay pot covered with muslin to dry in the sun. After a few days, the paste is ready. The locals call this *beltes* or *tomatozoumi*.

This recipe makes a relatively small quantity of sauce or paste. You can double or triple the amount; just remember that the boiling time will vary based on the tomatoes used and their water content. I prefer to keep the sauce neutral to avoid limiting its later use, however, you can flavour the sauce with garlic, herbs or spices by adding them during the first stage of boiling, and then straining them out.

To make the tomato sauce, blanch the tomatoes in boiling water and dry them with a clean dish towel. Cut each tomato in half and remove the seeds. Grate (shred) the tomato flesh into a bowl. Discard the skins. Place the tomatoes in a sieve (strainer) and sprinkle with salt. Leave to sit for 20–30 minutes to drain.

Transfer the drained tomatoes to a saucepan and place over a low heat. Gently simmer the tomatoes, stirring occasionally, for about 1½ hours or until the tomatoes have reduced significantly – adjust the cooking time until the sauce is your preferred consistency. Once thickened, you can either leave the sauce quite textured or refine it further. If you prefer a smooth sauce, use a handheld stick (immersion) blender or food processor to blitz it until smooth.

To make the tomato paste, follow the instructions for the tomato sauce but blend the tomatoes thoroughly using a handheld stick (immersion) blender. Continue to boil the tomatoes for 3½–4 hours over a very low heat, ensuring all the moisture evaporates and the mixture reduces and thickens to a paste.

Carefully scrape the tomato sauce or paste into a sterilised jar and seal tightly. To ensure a proper seal, invert the jar and leave it sat upside down for 15 minutes. Once cooled to room temperature, sprinkle a small amount of salt or pour a little olive oil over the surface of the sauce or paste for better preservation and to prevent mould. Store the jar in a cool, dark place.

Lemonada **Fresh lemonade with basil or mint**

FROM **POROS**

MAKES 800ML (27FL OZ)

500g (1lb 2oz) granulated sugar
Zest from 1 lemon (unwaxed)
2–3 fresh basil or mint sprigs
560ml (19fl oz) fresh lemon juice, strained

On the map, Poros seems to have drifted away from the north-eastern Peloponnese, separated by a narrow strait that's a five-minute boat ride from Galatas. This charming town has deep historical connections to Poros. It was a revered site for worshipping Poseidon, and you can still visit the ruins of his sanctuary on the island's northern side.

Lemons are integral to Poros, where the climate is perfect for growing citrus. Since antiquity, Poros lemons have been prized, with historical records showing they were exported to Constantinople and Smyrna. Poros is particularly famous for Lemonodasos, the 'lemon forest' – although officially part of Poros, it is located just across the strait in Galatas. Within this enchanting forest, thousands of fragrant lemon trees mix with olive and pomegranate. During the season, the air fills with the scent of citrus blossoms – it's no wonder Lemonodasos has inspired Greek folklore.

Lemons also play a key role in Greek cuisine. At most tavernas, dishes come with lemon wedges, and Greeks generously squeeze them over almost everything, adding a bright, tangy flavour that really enhances the taste. One of my favourite treats is freshly made lemonade, especially when lemons are in season and there's a need to preserve them and use them up while they are fresh. I love how it's served at cafes around Poros and other Greek islands, often with herbs added in it such as basil and mint or spices like *mastiha* and ginger. It's the perfect drink for a hot summer day – there's nothing like that zesty, cooling burst of flavour to keep you refreshed.

Combine the sugar, lemon zest and your choice of basil or mint sprigs in a large pot and pour in 280ml (9½fl oz) water. Place the pan over a medium heat and bring the mixture to a gentle boil. Once boiling, reduce the heat to low and let it simmer for 3 minutes, or just long enough for the sugar to dissolve completely. Remove the pan from the heat and let the mixture cool completely, leaving the herbs to infuse their flavours.

Once cooled, strain out the herbs and mix in the fresh lemon juice. Pour the lemonade into glass bottles. When stored in the fridge, the lemonade will keep for up to 2–3 months.

When you're ready to enjoy your lemonade, give the bottle a good shake to mix everything well. Mix one part of your homemade lemonade with two parts of chilled still or sparkling water, adjusting it to your taste. Serve over ice for a refreshing treat that's perfect for any occasion.

Fatourada **Liqueur with cinnamon, clove and orange**

FROM **KYTHIRA**

MAKES 700ML (24FL OZ)

Rind of 1 orange (unwaxed)
500ml (17fl oz) *tsipouro*, vodka or other mild flavoured distillate
4 cinnamon sticks
3 cloves
300g (10½oz) granulated sugar

Kythira is a truly enchanting island. Although it belongs to the Eptanisa group of Ionian Islands, it is closer to the Aegean and southern tip of the Peloponnese. Its location gives Kythira a distinctive character, blending the best of both island groups. The northern and central parts are characterised by fertile farmland and olive groves. These areas thrive with almond trees, artichokes, broad (fava) beans and a local variety of peach known as Aphrodite's breast, which is made into a spoon sweet. In contrast, the southern parts of the island, particularly the coast, are arid and rocky with less vegetation. However, this area is abundant in wild herbs and aromatic plants. Kythira's cuisine is a blend of Ionian and Aegean influences. The island is abundant in fish and seafood, offering dishes such as lobster pasta and *bourdeto*, as well as quail soup and stews with snails. The island's hand-collected summer salt is particularly famous, and it also produces delicious wheat rusks made with local olive oil.

Kythira is renowned for its vibrant festivals, including a famous one dedicated to wine. A highlight of Kythira's culinary tradition is *fatourada*, the island's famous liqueur. Crafted with *tsipouro* (which locals call *tsipoura*) made from locally grown grapes, *fatourada* is infused with cinnamon, cloves and often citrus rinds and other fruits, such as mandarins, oranges or apricots. This liqueur makes a great digestive and used to be a recipe prepared only in wealthier households. It's usually served straight or over ice and pairs wonderfully with fresh fruit or a simple dessert like dark chocolate mousse. You can try adding a splash to black tea for a spiced-up twist! If you wish to make it lighter, increase the amount of water in the syrup up to 500ml (18fl oz).

Wash the orange. Using a vegetable peeler, remove the rind from the orange in thick strips. With a knife, carefully cut away any white pith attached to the rind.

Place the *tsipouro* or vodka in a glass jar with a tight seal. Add the cinnamon sticks, cloves and orange rind. Seal tightly and store the jar in a cool, dark place for 15 days to allow the flavours to infuse.

Once 15 days have passed, prepare the syrup. Place the sugar in a heavy-based pan and pour in 200ml (7fl oz) water. Bring the mixture to a boil, then let it simmer over a medium–low heat for 5 minutes. Remove the pan from the heat and allow the syrup to cool completely.

Once the syrup has cooled, strain the *tsipouro* from the jar through a sieve (strainer) to remove the orange rind and whole spices. Pour the strained *tsipouro* back into the jar, followed by the syrup. Mix well. Seal the jar and store it in a cool, dark place for a further 15 days or longer, allowing the flavours to develop further.

Elies sto ladi **Easy marinades for green and black olives**

FROM **LESVOS**

Olive trees, much like vines, flourish across the Greek islands, though some may not yield large crops. Nearly half of the country's olive oil production comes from the islands, especially the larger ones like Crete, Evia, Lesvos, Samos, Corfu and Kefalonia. But even smaller, drier islands like Kea and the tiny Antiparos produce excellent olive oils using traditional methods. These islands often work with wild olive trees that require minimal water and produce olives that are rich in antioxidants.

Olives themselves are immensely popular and feature in many recipes, especially salads. While meatier olives are usually preferred, in Crete and other islands, locals enjoy the tiny olives typically used for oil. Although these olives hardly carry any flesh, they are a delightful snack with local distilled spirits, often resulting in a pile of tiny pits! On Thasos in the north, the famous Throuba olive is grown – a delightful, wrinkly black olive that is picked when very mature. On Lesvos, the local Kolovi olive is an exception; it is meaty and also used in olive oil production. Kolovi olives are picked both green (unripe) and black (ripe) for table olives.

When preparing olives at home, they are usually scored with a knife to speed up the curing process and enhance their flavour. After soaking in a salt water solution for several days, the olives are stored in brine, vinegar or olive oil, often infused with local herbs, citrus, garlic and spices.

Here are two easy marinades to spice up your olives at home. You can use them with any kind of olive you like or even a mix of different olives. Preserving olives this way not only makes them more delicious but also helps them last longer. It's important to use plain, unmarinated olives that are either air-packed or stored in brine. The olive oil from these marinades, if not too old, can be reused for fresh olives. It can also be used in recipes, such as salads or simple olive oil and garlic pasta. Since this oil is already infused with flavours, it can really elevate quick and simple dishes, making them utterly delicious.

MARINADE FOR GREEN OLIVES

- 250g (9oz) plain olives (not marinated with herbs or spices), air-packed or in brine
- ½ small lemon (unwaxed), halved and thinly sliced
- 1 small garlic clove, left whole
- 2 fresh thyme sprigs
- 2 bay leaves
- ½ teaspoon fennel seeds
- 300ml (10fl oz) olive oil

Rinse the olives thoroughly in cold running water, then drain well. Using a paring knife, lightly score the olives on one side and place them in a large, sterilised jar. Add the lemon slices and mix well. Tuck the garlic, herbs and fennel seeds into the jar, then pour in enough olive oil to cover the olives – they must be fully submerged to avoid spoiling. Store the jar in a cool, dry place (not the fridge).

MARINADE FOR BLACK OLIVES

- 250g (9oz) plain olives (not marinated with herbs or spices), air-packed or in brine
- 3 tablespoons red wine vinegar
- 2 thin slivers of orange zest (unwaxed)
- 2 fresh rosemary sprigs
- 1 fresh oregano sprig
- 5–7 whole black peppercorns
- 300ml (10fl oz) olive oil

Rinse the olives thoroughly in cold running water, then drain well. Using a paring knife, lightly score the olives on one side and place them in a large, sterilised jar. Pour in the vinegar and let the olives stand for 1–2 hours. Tuck the orange zest, herbs and peppercorns into the jar, then pour in enough olive oil to cover the olives – they must be fully submerged to avoid spoiling. Store the jar in a cool, dry place (not the fridge).

Marmelada Syko **Fig and black pepper jam**

FROM **CORFU**

MAKES 1 X 300ML (10FL OZ) JAR

500g (1lb 2oz) fresh figs
½ teaspoon fennel seeds (optional)
180g (6oz) brown sugar
4 teaspoons fresh lemon juice
60ml (2fl oz) fresh orange juice
Zest from 1 orange (unwaxed)
½–¾ teaspoon freshly ground black pepper (add more, if you like it spicier)

The abundant figs that grow on the islands make for excellent preserves, a common treat you'll often find on breakfast tables along with fresh, crusty bread, butter, other homemade jams and honey. For this recipe, I drew inspiration from the traditional *sykomaides* of Corfu, a type of spiced fig salami that is dried and sliced to serve as a meze with ouzo or tsipouro. *Sykomaida* traditionally includes pressed grapes and spices such as black pepper, fennel seeds and often ouzo. Corfiots sometimes use a bit of their *spetseriko* spice mix (see page 80–2) to enhance the flavour of *sykomaida*. In my version, I keep it simple, spicing the jam with orange zest, black pepper and a touch of fennel seeds, to pair well with both sweet and savoury dishes and as a spread on bread and butter. This jam is perfect with cheese, especially tangy, French-style white goat cheeses and blue cheeses like *kariki* from Tinos, gorgonzola, Roquefort and Stilton.

First, prepare the figs. Soak them in hot water for 5 minutes to soften, then drain and gently pat dry with a clean dish cloth. Remove the stems, then chop the figs, leaving the skins on for added texture and flavour.

Meanwhile, using a mortar and pestle, finely grind the fennel seeds to release their aroma.

Combine the chopped figs with a generous sprinkling of the sugar in a heavy-based pan with a lid. Add the lemon juice, orange juice and orange zest, along with the ground fennel seeds and black pepper. Cover the pan and let the figs sit for 2–3 hours to allow the flavours to mingle.

Place the pan over a medium heat and cook, stirring occasionally, until the figs break down which then reduces and thickens to your preferred jam consistency. To check if the jam is ready, drop a small spoonful onto a cold plate. If it sets nicely, the jam is done; if not, continue cooking the jam for a bit longer.

Carefully pour the hot jam into sterilised jars. Fill each jar almost to the top, leaving only about 0.5cm (¼ inch) of space at the rim. Seal the jars tightly and let them cool completely. Store the jars in a cool, dry place. Once opened, keep the jam in the fridge.

SWEET PRESERVES: *Jams, Spoon Sweets, Cordials and Liqueurs*

Fruits, nuts, vegetables and even edible flowers are commonly preserved as sweets. Traditionally, these sweets are made from foraged foods, surplus harvests or parts of a food that would otherwise be discarded, such as citrus rinds. Popular sweet preserves focus on ingredients such as citrus fruits, sour cherries, grapes, figs, almonds, pumpkins, tomatoes, rose petals, lemon blossoms and even watermelon rind and aubergines (eggplants).

Among the most popular preserves on the islands are apricot, mulberry, greengage plum, fig, quince and various citrus marmalades. Notable examples include the famous tangerine marmalade from a special Chios variety with a fantastic fragrance.

When the ingredients are preserved whole or in chunks in a syrup, the treat is called glyko tou koutaliou, which translates as 'spoon sweets'. These are served either plain or with yogurt, or to accompany desserts such as cheesecakes or rice pudding. When served plain, they are typically presented on a small plate with a teaspoon either as a whole fruit standing in the centre, such as a small wild fig or unripe bitter orange, or in teaspoon portions, holding a few pieces of fruit. This welcome treat is offered upon arrival at a Greek home, along with a coffee.

Some of the most famous island spoon sweets include small tomatoes from Nisiros, prunes from Skopelos preserved while unripe and yellow, and koufeto from Milos, made with chunky pumpkin pieces, whole blanched almonds and honey. On Syros, you find caper spoon sweets, while on Tinos, you can savour artichoke, both of which are unexpectedly delicious. On many islands, including Limnos, the white part of the watermelon rind is used after removing the bitter external green part. On Andros and Thasos, they use unripe whole green walnuts, before their shell has formed inside, spiced with whole cloves.

Sour cherries are used to make a popular liqueur and cordial known as visinada (see page 217). Similar cordials are made from almonds, like the renowned soumada of Lefkada, and citrus, mostly lemons and tangerines.

The variety of liqueurs made across the islands is vast and depends on what is available in each region. Special fruits star in these drinks, from the aromatic kumquat liqueur of Corfu to the citron liqueur of Naxos. Chios mastiha is another popular liqueur with digestive properties, commonly offered after dinner. Local island liqueurs also include honey, spices and herbs, such as rose geranium and spearmint. One notable example is the wonderful fatourada from Kythira, made with the local grape distillate, infused with cinnamon and cloves, and sometimes including fruit, most commonly mandarins or apricots.

All these preserves, cordials and liqueurs are testament to the resourcefulness and creativity of the islanders but also a charming tradition of philoxenia (hospitality). Offering these delightful treats is a warm way of welcoming guests and sharing a taste of local heritage.

Glyko Verikoko **Apricots preserved in syrup**

FROM **RHODES**

MAKES 2 X 300ML (10FL OZ) JARS

- 1kg (2lb 4oz) slightly under-ripe, firm apricots
- 30g (1oz) bicarbonate of soda (baking soda)
- 1kg (2lb 4oz) caster (superfine) sugar
- 1 vanilla pod (bean)
- 2 fresh rose geranium leaves (optional)
- 5–6 apricot kernels (found inside the stone/pit)
- Juice of 1 lemon (about 40ml/ 3 tablespoons)
- 1 thin sliver of lemon zest (unwaxed)

Apricots grow abundantly on many Greek islands, including Rhodes, Evia, Crete, Tinos, Ikaria and Naxos. Some local varieties grow wild in fields – they are bursting with flavour. To preserve their taste, apricots are dried, made into jams (preserves) or crafted into spoon sweets, just like in Afantos on Rhodes. This village is known for the fragrant Aegean apricot known as Kaisia, which was its main source of income before tourism took over. As well as making spoon sweets with under-ripe apricots, villagers create a sun-dried paste from the ripe fruit, similar to quince paste. Each summer, they host a festival to celebrate this beloved fruit, offering these local treats to visitors.

Apricots in syrup are one of my favourite spoon sweets; they capture the essence of Greek summers. Enjoyed with coffee or over creamy yogurt, this fruity spoonful lifts the spirits. For this recipe, use aromatic apricots that aren't fully ripe but are ripe enough to easily remove the stone (pit). Some cooks keep the apricots whole and stuff them with an almond for extra sweetness. I prefer to halve them and find that soaking them in bicarbonate of soda (baking soda) and adjusting the boiling time results in a sweet that is both tender and flavourful.

I add aromatic rose geranium leaves, which pair beautifully with apricots. Islanders often use rose geranium in sweet jams, as well as liqueurs and herbal teas. You can omit them or add other whole spices, such as cinnamon, cloves and even chillies.

Wash the apricots. Fill a large bowl with water and stir in the bicarbonate of soda (baking soda). Submerge the apricots in the water and leave to soak for 1 hour. Rinse, then drain well. Halve the apricots and remove the stones (pits).

Place the sugar in a heavy-based pan and pour in 500ml (17fl oz) water. Bring to the boil, then reduce the heat to medium and simmer for 2–3 minutes to dissolve the sugar. Add the apricots, bring to the boil, then gently simmer for 2–3 minutes. Using a slotted spoon, carefully transfer the apricots to a tray.

Add the vanilla pod (bean), geranium leaves, lemon juice and zest to the pan and simmer for 1 minute. To test if the syrup is ready, let a drop of the hot syrup fall into a glass of cold water. If the drop holds its shape as a ball or forms a pliable thread without dissolving immediately, the syrup is ready. If not, continue simmering and test again after a further 1 minute. Remove the pan from the heat and let the syrup cool down for 20 minutes.

Return the apricots to the syrup and leave to sit for 24 hours. The next day, transfer the apricots to sterilised jars, seal the jars and store in a cool, dark place.

After the apricots have been eaten, any syrup left in the jar can be drizzled over cakes, pancakes, ice cream and other sweet treats.

Visinada **Sour cherry cordial**

FROM **CHIOS**

MAKES ABOUT 1.5 LITRES (1.5 QUARTS)

1kg (2lb 4oz) sour cherries
550g (1lb 3½oz) granulated white sugar
70ml (2½fl oz) fresh lemon juice
Fresh mint sprigs (optional), to serve

Sour cherry trees are a common sight on many islands, often growing wild in fields. On Chios, these trees flourish both in the north of the island and the Kambos region, renowned for its citrus groves. Harvested in early summer, sour cherries are used in a variety of treats, including jams, spoon sweets and liqueurs. They are the star ingredient in *visinada*, an old-school cordial for summer refreshment. While making *visinada* is fun, it's messy. Try removing any stains with ouzo – it works like magic!

Visinada is versatile and can last for months (although you may finish it sooner). When served as a cool, refreshing drink, the cordial is diluted with water and poured over plenty of ice in tall glasses. In its undiluted form, *visinada* is a luscious syrup perfect for drizzling over desserts, such as pavlovas, cheesecakes, panna cottas and ice cream, especially the traditional Chios *mastiha* ice cream or yogurt ice cream. It's also excellent in cocktails, spritzes and punches in place of grenadine.

Wash the cherries and leave them to dry. Over a large pot, remove the stones (pits) from the cherries. You can use a special tool (pitter) or a long pin or hair pin. Simply press the pin into the centre of the cherry until the stone pops out.

To prepare the syrup, place the sugar in a heavy-based pan and pour in 200ml (7fl oz) water. Bring the mixture to a boil over a medium heat, then let it boil for 20 minutes or until thickened. To test if the syrup is ready, let a drop of the hot syrup fall into a glass of cold water. If the drop holds its shape as a ball or forms a pliable thread without dissolving immediately, the syrup is ready. If not, continue boiling and test again after a few more minutes.

Once the syrup reaches the desired consistency, add the cherries and lemon juice, stirring to distribute the fruit evenly. Skim off any foam that forms on the surface, and let the mixture boil for a further 10 minutes. Remove the pan from the heat and allow the mixture to cool slightly, letting the flavours combine.

Strain the cherry mixture through a sieve (strainer), pressing the fruit with a spoon or potato masher to extract as much pulp and juice as possible. Strain the sour cherry juice again, reserving any fruit that is left behind. (You can pass the cherries through the sieve one more time to achieve the ideal consistency.)

Transfer the cherry cordial into sterilised glass bottles. Once it has cooled, seal the bottles and store in the fridge. (Any leftover fruit can be blitzed in a food processor until smooth, then stored in a jar and used as a delicious preserve – it's fantastic spread on bread paired with almond butter.)

To serve the cordial as a drink, fill a tall glass one-third full with the cherry cordial, add plenty of ice and then top up with cold water. Stir to mix well. For extra freshness and aroma, add a fresh mint sprig to the glass.

Freddo at the beach

Ultimate Greek-style iced coffee

FROM **THE ISLANDS**

SERVES 1

- 1 double espresso
- Sugar (or your preferred sweetener), to taste
- Large ice cubes
- 60ml (2fl oz) cold semi-skimmed milk (from a carton)
- Ground cinnamon or unsweetened cocoa powder (optional)

Whether it's a frappé made with instant coffee or the more popular Freddo made with espresso, there's no better way to enjoy coffee on a hot day. Greeks truly are masters of iced coffee, crafting drinks that look like foamy, grande frappuccinos. In reality, they are mostly whipped milk with coffee, though there are many creative variations.

To achieve the perfect texture when whipping the milk, make sure it's well chilled. A skilled barista once told me to use fresh semi-skimmed milk from a carton because it turns creamier when whipped. He was right, so that's what I now use. You can use vegan milks, but they don't whip as well. Coconut cream, however, is a great alternative that adds a tropical twist. To turn it into an indulgent treat, add ice cream instead of milk. For best results, you need a metal cocktail shaker and high-powered milk frother.

Before you start, place the cup of the metal cocktail shaker in the freezer to chill while you prepare the ingredients.

Brew the coffee using your preferred method. If you're adding sugar or any other sweetener, stir it into the hot coffee until fully dissolved.

Next, fill a bowl with ice cubes and nestle the chilled metal shaker cup into the bowl. Pour the hot coffee into the metal shaker cup and whip with the milk frother to blend and cool it down.

Half fill a glass with large ice cubes (large enough so they don't melt too quickly), then pour the cooled coffee over the ice.

If you're making a Freddo cappuccino, quickly rinse and dry the shaker cup, then return it to the bowl of ice (refreshing the ice, if necessary). Pour the milk into the shaker cup and whip with the milk frother until thick and creamy.

Pour the whipped milk into the glass so that it sits on top of coffee. Sprinkle a little ground cinnamon or cocoa powder on top, if you like.

Index

ACKNOWLEDGEMENTS

I would like to express my heartfelt thanks to everyone who contributed to the creation of this book. My gratitude goes to all the people who generously shared with me their island traditions and stories. A special mention to Eleftheria Mamidaki, Kiki Vasalou and the Anoskeli Olive Oil and Winery in Crete; Irini Zouganeli from Mykonos; Charitatos Estate on Kefalonia along with Ioanna and Veroniki Charitatou; Kiki Sereti and Christina Vlachoulis from Kefalonia; Christina Loverdou from Ithaca; Melina Livitsanou from Lefkada; Moraitis Winery in Paros; Zad Mehdawi, Zoe Xemantilotou, Alkis Downward and Petra Farm on Paros; Petros and Brigitte and Noé Ceramics on Paros; the Farmers' Cooperative Union on Paros, particularly Markos Kortianos; Agrilia Estate on Antiparos, Marilita and Daphne Lambadarios, Dimitris, Maria, Daphne and Mathias; Eleni Theodorou and Anna Vidou from Tinos; Eleftheria and Katia Farid from Chois; Maro Narli from Sifnos; Eugenia Markesini-Hobson and her son Alex; Gina Moskonas-Malta and her daughter Fani; and Eleni Harou and Irini Manolakou from Kythira. I am eternally grateful to Manos Chatzikonstantis for his incredible photography, positivity and patience, as well as the wonderful support from his wife, Eirini Rapti. A huge thank you to Carly Martin-Gammon for always being there for me and ready to test yet another recipe. Special thanks to Céline Hughes, Lisa Pendreigh and the entire Murdoch Books team for their hard work and love in bringing this book to life. A very big thanks to Lucy Sykes-Thompson at Studio Polka for her amazing work on the book design. And thanks to Rotzer Fiser for loaning many of the beautiful props used throughout this book. Finally, a big thanks to my dear son Apollo, who is always eager to taste anything and analyse flavours with the insight of a true foodie.

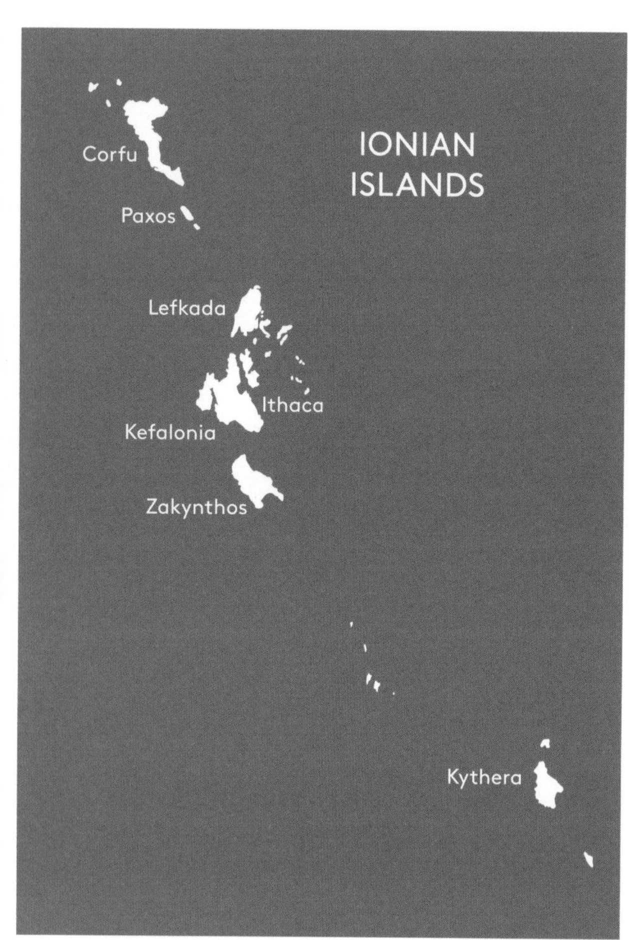
IONIAN
ISLANDS
Corfu
Paxos
Lefkada
Ithaca
Kefalonia
Zakynthos
Kythera

Salamina
Aegina
SARONIC
ISLANDS
Poros
Hydra
Spetses

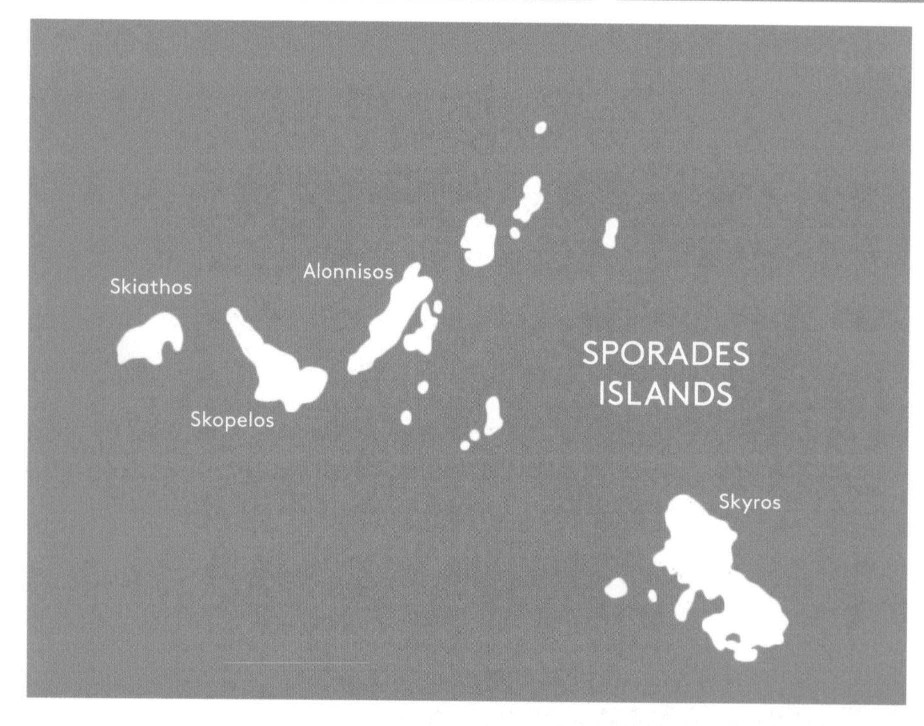
Skiathos
Alonnisos
SPORADES
ISLANDS
Skopelos
Skyros